W9-AEW-442

ILLUMINATIONS

BOA Editions
New American Translation Series

Vol. 1: *Illuminations*
Poems by Arthur Rimbaud
Translated by Bertrand Mathieu
Foreword and Lithograph by Henry Miller

ILLUMINATIONS
ARTHUR RIMBAUD

a new American translation by
BERTRAND MATHIEU
with foreword and lithograph by
HENRY MILLER

WITHDRAWN

BOA EDITIONS • BROCKPORT NEW YORK • 1979

Grateful acknowledgment is made to the editors of *The American Poetry Review* in which an earlier version of this translation of Rimbaud's *Illuminations* first appeared.

The publication of these translations of Rimbaud's *Illuminations* was made possible with the assistance of a grant from the National Endowment for the Arts in Washington, D.C., a Federal agency.

The translator and the publisher are grateful to Henry Miller and to Gary Koeppel of the Coast Gallery for permission to reproduce "Clownesque," the lithograph by Henry Miller from the S. Kubo Collection.

Illuminations by Arthur Rimbaud. Translation copyright ©1973, 1978 by Bertrand Mathieu. Foreword and watercolors, copyright ©1978 by Henry Miller. All rights reserved. Printed in the United States of America. Except in case of brief quotations in reviews and critical articles, no part of this publication may be reproduced or transmitted in any form or by any means, electronic or mechanical, including photocopy, recording, or any information storage and retrieval system, without permission in writing from the publisher. All inquiries should be addressed to A. Poulin, Jr., BOA Editions, 92 Park Avenue, Brockport, New York, 14420.

Printed at the Visual Studies Workshop.
Designed by Janet Zweig.
Typeset by Advertising and Marketing Graphics.
Binding by Gene Eckert, Inc.
Distributed by the Book Bus, Visual Studies Workshop
31 Prince Street, Rochester, New York 14607.

ISBN 0-918526-15-9 Cloth
      0-918526-16-7 Paper

First edition: January, 1979

For Russell and Rachel

780626 - 4R cig
81/03/24

CONTENTS

FOREWORD

It was exactly fifty years ago, in a basement apartment in
Brooklyn in 1927, that I first heard the name of Arthur
Rimbaud. I was destined to give a lot of attention to the
life and writings of this amazing human phenomenon in
years to come, but that summer there was another boyish
"hero" who was eclipsing Rimbaud all over America and
all over the rest of the world. I speak of Charles A.
Lindbergh, the "Lone Eagle," who had just made his solo
flight across the Atlantic to Rimbaud's own France.

In retrospect, how *insignificant* the flight of "The Spirit of
Saint Louis" now seems in comparison with the audacious
solo flights of mind of the boy-poet from Charleville!
And how much more impressive a figure Rimbaud now
cuts than the loudly adulated pilot of 1927. But, *comme
d'habitude,* the world reserved its ticker-tape parades and
all its dizzy-headed hoopla for the acrobat who had per-
formed his feats *in public,* whereas the infinitely more
risky private stunts of the imagination performed by such
a one as Rimbaud earned him merely the scorn of the
public and, in the end, an unbelievably painful death in a
Marseilles hospital after the amputation of a gangrenous
leg acquired during the poet's embittered exile in Africa.
Icarus himself — as hungry as Rimbaud had been for the
sun — was not so cruelly used by the gods!

11

Frankly, I find Rimbaud's *Illuminations* the most baffling of all Rimbaud's works, either rhymed or unrhymed. But what Bertrand Mathieu has done in these transparent new American versions of this work makes absolute sense to me. In reality, Rimbaud's writings have always seemed to me to be a *total mystery* — as mysterious as love, as sunlight, as the flight of birds. But perhaps as *simple* as these things are also. And Bert Mathieu has managed to translate all of the baffling simplicity and incandescence of Rimbaud's originals into a vivid American idiom which should speak *directly* to our own moment.

There is no doubt in my mind that Rimbaud's life-expanding vision of things has never been more desperately needed than it is today. It has been lying in wait for us all along. ("We die of hunger while sitting by the rice bag," as one wise old Japanese poet has put it.) I say we need more Rimbauds and fewer Lindberghs! These *Illuminations* should be especially appealing to today's young readers, who in my opinion are spiritually undernourished by what their eyes are offered daily by the boob tube. We are *all* very much in need of the kind of visual dynamite which Rimbaud packed into the originals of his great poems. These wonderfully readable new versions of the *Illuminations* have something in them that is truly remarkable. Through them, Rimbaud can clearly be heard speaking to us once again!

Henry Miller

Henry Miller
Pacific Palisades, California
Summer 1977

SEVEN PARAGRAPHS
ON RIMBAUD AND *ILLUMINATIONS*

Rimbaud's *Illuminations* is one of the most powerfully
influential masterpieces of our era, yet no one knows to
this day what the exact sequence of its 42 poems should
be. The standard French edition, published by Gallimard,
follows the order recommended by Rimbaud's friend and
fellow-vagabond, Paul Verlaine. But the messy bundle
of manuscripts that Rimbaud turned over to Verlaine in
Stuttgart in 1875, right after Rimbaud had decided to give
up poetry for good, was unedited, uncorrected, unfinished.
Verlaine didn't really know what ultimate design
Rimbaud had in mind for *Illuminations*. And even though
he could have written to the world-wandering Rimbaud in
later years to find out, he never did. By the time *Illumin-
ations* was first published in the French magazine *La
Vogue* in 1886, more than ten years had gone by since
Rimbaud had stopped writing poems. In his frenetic
eagerness to "escape from poetry," Rimbaud had already
enlisted in the Dutch colonial army in Batavia and
deserted, joined a grubby circus headed for Scandinavia
in Hamburg, crossed the Alps on foot and nearly froze to
death in a violent snowstorm, worked as a builder's fore-
man in Cyprus during a summer of record-breaking heat,
and had worn himself out as a trader in the hell-holes of
Aden and Harar in North Africa (coffee, gum, ivory,
hides, guns, slaves). When this dying dromomaniac
returned to Europe at the age of 37, he completely cut

himself off from literary circles. His fans in Paris were
calling him "the late Arthur Rimbaud," believing he had
died in Abyssinia a few years earlier. At the end, one
man — his physician, Dr. Beaudier, who knew about
Rimbaud's growing fame in Paris and the numberless
enigmas surrounding his work — tried to ask the poet a
few questions. But Rimbaud wouldn't talk. As he tor-
mentedly inched his way towards death on the farm of his
miserly mother in Roche near Charleville (his cancerous
right leg amputated, his left knee hideously swollen from
the effects of carcinoma, his whole body tortured by
ceaseless insomnia and fever), Rimbaud snapped back at
the doctor: "Please cut it out! I'm *through* with all that
shit."

2

The sequence of the *Illuminations* isn't the only thing
Verlaine got wrong. His brief note, accompanying the first
publication of these incandescent prose poems, insists that
Rimbaud got the idea for his title from some illuminated
medieval manuscripts which they had examined together
at the British Museum during their London trip in 1872.
This preposterously one-sided notion has been repeated
often and has caused generations of Rimbaud's readers to
miss the poems' crucially *magical* dimension. Verlaine's
biographers have had a harder time than most because of
their subject's notoriously bad memory, but by 1886 (they
all agree on this) the brain of "pauvre Lélian" was quite
completely befuddled with guilt and absinthe. Verlaine
had by now forgotten the dream he had once dreamed
with the young "voyant" in squalid rented rooms "full
of dirty daylight and spider noises" where, with the savage
assertiveness of his radiant god-like presence, Rimbaud
had outlined his fantastic self-ordained mission to "change
life itself" by means of a totally new kind of language, by
means of magic. Enid Starkie's researches into the life of

Rimbaud have proved conclusively that Rimbaud had made a profound study of occult and illuminist philosophy. We know he had access to the writings of Swedenborg and Eliphas Lévi in his teens. There's evidence that he had devoured such works as Franck's *Histoire de la Kabbale* (1843) and Lévi's *L'Histoire de la Magie (1860)* and *Les Clefs des Grands Mystères* (1861), that he had read and been blasted by Balzac's ecstatic/illuminist novels, *Séraphita* and *Louis Lambert*. His famous "seer letters" of May 1871 are full of illuminist doctrine with its elliptical insolence, full of a terrific thirst for god-like powers. The real poet, he writes to Paul Demeny, "makes himself a SEER by a long, immense, and reasoned derangement of ALL THE SENSES" in order to become the instrument of higher powers that long to speak through him. The poet can transfigure the drab "real" world into the paradise that shimmers, precariously, right under the skin of mere brute appearance. *This* is what Rimbaud means by "illuminations." An "illuminist" is a person who can transmit light because he enjoys and possesses light himself. Rimbaud knew that occulists have always taken the sun to be the symbol of universal creative energy. Swedenborg says that God appears in the heavens as the sun because he is the Divine Love by which all things of the spirit exist, just as by means of this solar light all natural things exist. When a seer has transformed himself into pure light and has placed his own mortal will in direct touch with the voice-tones of divinity, his words will be magically transmuted into a luminous new kind of language that will change life itself! His powers are now unlimited because he has become one with divinity. He's now a creator in his own right and can control natural forces. He has dominion over birds, fish, flowers, animals, storms, geography, events. The first duty of man, according to Lévi, is to perceive *fully* the significance of what he's able to experience and to *utter* (to "utter" is to "make *outer*"). Then humanity will glow in the dark like the stars and the angels. *That's* the burden Rimbaud was laying on Verlaine in "Vagabonds," one of the most "doctrine"-filled poems of *Illuminations*: "I'd made a vow, in absolute sincerity, to bring him back again to his primitive state of son of the Sun."

3

A Sunday morning in 1862. Charleville, a provincial French town on the Belgian border. Arthur Rimbaud is 8 years old. The Rimbaud family is setting off for High Mass and the neighbors, knowing what's coming, are poking their heads like clockwork out of the windows, along the way, to gape at this strange procession. First the two little daughters, Vitalie and Isabelle, hand in hand, with their clean white cotton gloves and their shining black buttoned boots. Then the two brothers Frédéric and Arthur, in their black jackets and slate-blue trousers, their round white collars and their funny little black bowler hats, each carrying a bright blue cotton umbrella. Finally, Madame Rimbaud bringing up the rear — walking alone, in her inflexible dignity, as rigid as a Prussian field-marshal, dressed in blackest black from top to toe, "in mourning" for her "dead" husband who had actually walked out on her one day and was never seen again. Years later, her son would write that when "la mère Rimb" made up her mind it was "like 73 civic administrations wearing pointed leaden helmets." But for the time being, he stifles his curses and wears endless pairs of trousers made of that slate-blue material, throughout his school years, because his mother had once bought a huge roll of the stuff, cheap, at a clearance sale. She's a tall, thin woman, unbelievably hard and severe — on Sundays, especially — with the gnarled, knotted hands of her peasant father and peasant grandfather before him. A mouth sharp as a knife's edge. A style of terrific authori-

tarian heaviness that tolerates no backtalk, no contradic-
tion, no appeal. Not a trace of warmth — the type of
mother that breeds psychopathic killers, misogynists,
and other absolutists. Rimbaud suffered indescribable
torments at her hands, as *Illuminations* and *A Season in
Hell* both testify, yet like other occultists he envisions a
crucial and dignified role for women in the future. In
Histoire de la Magie, Eliphas Lévi had written: "Woman
is the queen of harmony and that is why she must be at
the head of the regenerating movement of the future.
Woman is higher on the scale of love than man and when
love comes to the fore, then woman will be the queen
of the universe." Rimbaud openly borrows Lévi's meta-
phors in "Dawn," "Spells," "Fairyland," "Cities I," but
most marvelously in the short poem "Royalty", luminous
and flawlessly beautiful. Before starting work on *Illumina-
tions,* he had written to Paul Demeny: "When the endless
servitude of woman is smashed, when she lives for and
by herself, man — heretofore abominable — having given
her her release, she *too* will be a poet! Woman will dis-
cover some of the unknown! Will her world of ideas
differ from ours? — She will find strange, unfathomable,
repulsive, delicious things: we will take them, we will
understand them." Rimbaud had made up his mind long
before Women's Liberation had made it a plank in its
platform that both men and women must lose some of
their avoirdupois, become light. Light as thunderbolts.
"Life's *got* to be changed!"

4

The language of Rimbaud's *Illuminations* is a special
problem. Everyone recognizes that these strangely
glimmerous/hermetic prose poems which Rimbaud wrote
before he was 20 years old, along with Nerval's *Les
Chimères* and Baudelaire's *Les Fleurs du Mal,* are abso-
lutely inseparable from what's most vital and most

exciting in modern French poetry. Rimbaud unquestion-
ably achieved his most astonishing feats of creative
originality in the prose poem, a form which he radically
re-made to suit his programmatic ambitions. Rimbaud saw
himself as a magus violently bent on stripping the mask
of falseness off the face of "reality" by stripping language
itself of its inherited rhetorical clutter (rhyme, meter,
anecdote, description, "content"). To Rimbaud poetry was
merely a means to an end, and it's next to impossible to
understand Breton, Tzara, Claudel, St. John Perse, and
Eluard (not to mention Hart Crane and Henry Miller here
in the States) unless one understands this. The *Illumina-
tions* are celebrations of perpetual *amazement* at the in-
credible brightness of things. Each of the poems is its
own verbal universe, its own paradise (the etymology of
"paradise" is from *pairi* "around" and *daeza* "wall," i.e.,
an enclosed area, a place completely walled off from all
other places). Though certain themes recur in the
series — ecstasy, blood, anguish, walking, love, gigan-
tism — no single poem really depends on the others or
counts on them to achieve its own perfections. Each is
intrinsic. (We don't know the exact sequence and we
don't *need* to know it.) Each is "inexplicable," each is a
miracle of separateness which, paradoxically, is designed
to give us a blazing fragment of insight and not the whole
picture all at once. Occult writers always emphasize the
importance of words *in themselves* — their unique shapes,
their sounds, their autonomous beauty. All magi believe
that the word and its total signification are so completely
one that if language were effectively used, no explanatory
words or clauses would be needed. The single word,
perfectly chosen, would be enough to contain all and
reveal all (*cf.* "The Aleph" by the Argentinian magus
Jorge Luis Borges for a good recent example). Much of
the supposed obscurity of Rimbaud's poetry disappears as
soon as the reader becomes aware that he's face to face

with an awesomely nimble cabalist, a sleight-of-hand artist
who can create heavens and hells, or annihilate them, with
equal ease. Analogies explain nothing, but perhaps
Rimbaud's *Illuminations* can best be understood in terms
of an ingenious kaleidoscope. The weirdly contrived
phrases and clauses — fragments of colored glass and
jewelry, oddments of flesh and nightmare and blood-
smeared bone — are carefully arranged by the kaleido-
scopist's hand to enchant your eye. But as soon as the
entire picture fills the eye-line, a tap of the poet's
finger makes everything collapse. Most of the *Illumina-
tions* leave you thus empty-handed and full of amazement.
You know you've been struck by lightning but there's
nothing (not even the pieces) left to prove it. One more
analogy, perhaps: the pantomimist Marcel Marceau can
blow your mind by leaning casually, comfortably, on
nothing. But Rimbaud, by nature a walker, knows how to
take vividly effortless somnambulistic strolls *in mid-air.*

5

My own ambitions in this new American version of *Illu-
minations* are: to remain strictly faithful to Rimbaud's
anarchist/psychedelic vision of reality; to eliminate a
great number of linguistic bloopers and outright distor-
tions that have weakened previous English renderings of
the work; and to construct a long poem that will recreate
the terrifying excitements and verbal ingenuities of
Illuminations in a readable "American idiom" equivalent.
I've tried especially hard to find exact American equi-
valents (exact both in sound and sense) to match the
incredible crackle and glow of Rimbaud's "voyou" lingo.
Let my translation of "Départ" serve as an illustration. In
the existing English versions of the poem, the word
"départ" in the title and closing line of the original is
rendered "departure." Now "departure" is all wrong for

Rimbaud. That word's acquired rather formal connotations in English that Rimbaud wouldn't have wanted. A university president or an archbishop might resort to such a word, but not this brilliant little punk/angel with his hair full of lice, with his record for sleeping under more bridges at night than any French poet since François Villon. For us "departure" carries rather restrictive connotations (e.g., the President's "departure" for the summer White House). Or train "departures." Rimbaud could never afford trains and when he took them, he always tried to bail out before the ticket collector came along. "The man with heels of wind," as Verlaine called him. An obsessional walker. "Cutting out" is the only locution I can think of that has the crispness of the French word and Rimbaud's own slangy bluntness. Other particulars in that poem: "à tous les airs" in the first line is always translated "in all airs," but that's idiomatically a bit ridiculous. What Rimbaud is saying is "in all kinds of weather" or "in season and out". The latter alternative is particularly attractive since there's new evidence that *A Season in Hell* was not in fact Rimbaud's "farewell to literature," that many of the *Illuminations* (perhaps including "Départ") were merely farewells to the kind of descent into horror — or *katábasis* — that he'd been doing in *Une Saison en Enfer*. In addition, using "season" in the first line preserves the deft alliterations Rimbaud regularly uses in his not-really-prose lines. My "seen" and "season" match his "assez" and "s'est," for instance: my "vision bumped into" and "in season and out" melopoeically approximate his "rencontrée" and "tous les airs." There are hundreds of parallel attempts to reconstruct Rimbaud's subtle and elusive music throughout my versions. (Hopefully, some of them work.) But it's not only their melodic colorlessness that make earlier versions of *Illuminations* hard to take. Their impossible diction and word choices often date them, also. They characteristically

20

use words like "promontory" instead of "headland," "subsided" instead of "simmered down," "beauteous" instead of "beautiful," "dispersed" instead of "scattered," etc. They tend to opt for the mandarin level of usage, whereas Rimbaud himself has been the inspiration of French poets from Verlaine to Francis Ponge for the delight he takes in the direct, the scatalogical, the *gutsy*.

6

English and American translators of *Illuminations* have been culpably timid in dealing with Rimbaud's special brand of coarseness. His hellish bad luck in life left deep wounds in his language and these must be retained in the language of the translator if American readers are to understand the view of "heaven" the poet offers. (Rimbaud is known to have been raped, brutally, by tobacco-chewing National Guardsmen during the Paris Commune of 1872). The poem "Side Show" dramatizes Rimbaud's pederastic nightmare in a ferociously direct way, despite the teasing obscurantism. The rank smell of sodomy penetrates even the most innocent "descriptive" phrasings in the poem. The last sentence of Rimbaud's first paragraph reads: "On les envoie prendre du dos en ville, affublés d'un luxe dégoûtant." The French argot "prendre du dos" means, quite simply, "buggering, fucking from the rear" — and it's obvious from the context that a violent homoeroticism between men is involved. Yet Louise Varèse translates this: "They are *sent snaring* in the town, tricked out with nauseating luxury." Wallace Fowlie elegantly shirks the whole thing by rendering it: "They are *sent to the city for trade,* decked out in disgusting finery." What Rimbaud is *really* saying is: "They send these studs to town *to bugger,* decked out in revolting duds." Another poem in which Varèse and Fowlie are cautious to the point of blurriness is "H". This is a poem

about Rimbaud's masturbation fantasies — he was an 18-
or 19-year old kid who had never been laid and Hortense
is clearly a tantalizing figment of his imagination that
gives him great pleasure and great guilt. The closing
words of the poem make it clear that Rimbaud is inviting
"discovery" of his sin (and of the secret of his poetic
inventiveness) by turning the whole thing, abruptly, into
a guessing game, a charade. But much of the poignancy of
Rimbaud's (admittedly "mystifying") poem is lost in the
soft, almost Victorian wording of the Varèse and Fowlie
translations. There's an uncannily prophetic quality to *some*
of the political poems in *Illuminations,* also, which ought
to be brought out for present-day readers in an updated
translation. "Democracy," for instance. It sounds as if
Rimbaud is describing Vietnam and the events of 1967-
68 in the American ghettos, doesn't it? Look again. The
poem was prompted by the Franco-Prussian débâcle of
1871! ("The seer-poet knows the meaning of the past, the
present, and the future. The secret of the resurrection of
the dead and the keys of immortality are in his hands . . .
When a great genius prophesies, he is only in reality
remembering a sensation he has experienced, for the
future is in the past, the past is in the future, and every-
thing is in him." Eliphas Lévi, *Histoire de la Magie,*
p. 542 & 544.) Another of these "prophetic" poems is
"Turned-On Morning," which Rimbaud calls "Matinée
d'Ivresse" but which Varèse and Fowlie give us as "Morn-
ing of Drunkenness," despite the smell of hashish that
hovers over the whole poem. Look at the closing line:
"Now's the time of the ASSASSINS." The word "assassin"
is derived from "hashishin," a smoker of hash, and
Rimbaud (who was smoking hash in the early 1870's) was
fully aware of this. This poem describes Rimbaud's feel-
ings of anguished disillusionment in the wake of the fail-
ure of the Paris Commune, in which he'd taken part.
His feelings of solidarity with the Paris proletariat were

intense (*cf.* "Workers") and the crushing of the Commune by the reactionaries was one of the great death-blows to his spirit. At the peak of his involvement in the Commune, he was sure the Revolution (the "New Sound") was here to stay. How accurately "Turned-On Morning" delineates our own nihilistic sense of later betrayals in Chicago (1968) and the numb helpless fury that gripped the brain after the Nixonite "landslide" of 1972, the squelching of the "Revolution" here in the States. But that's neither here nor there. Whether our bodies live or die, Rimbaud's poems will continue to devote their energies to our well-being, night and day, while the ravenous centaurs keep an eye on us from the corner newsstands.

7

Rimbaud wrote devastatingly about his political and spiritual disappointments in *A Season in Hell,* but worse things were in store for him during the 17 years he had left to live after giving up poetry. He stopped writing but remained an absolutist. His roamings all over the earth are incredible. His death was more nightmarish than anything his own imagination could have invented, pure horror. Here's how the last phase began: In October, 1878, Rimbaud met a man who promised him a job in Egypt if he would go right away to Genoa to take the boat about to leave from there for Alexandria. He traveled the length of France but discovered when he reached Altdorf that the pass across the Alps was closed to traffic for the winter and that, in order to reach Italy, he'd have to cross the mountains on foot. He took off in a violent snowstorm — *on foot!* From Altdorf the road quickly became a wind-lashed labyrinth, rising steeper and steeper. Snowdrifts six feet high often blocked the road, and he had to dig his way through while huge hailstones hit him in the face. There wasn't a shadow to be

seen after a long while, no precipices, no mountains,
nothing but a blinding whiteness freezing his body, his
eyes, his consciousness. He couldn't take his eyes off
the blinding whiteness, no matter where he turned. His
eyelashes, eyebrows, moustache were crusted with ice, his
ears flayed by the wind, his neck swollen from the effort
of climbing. There was nothing to help him stick to the
road except an occasional telegraph pole (the wires over-
head were completely invisible in the all-dazzling white-
ness). At one point in his climb he had to dig his way
through a snowdrift three feet deep, along the length of a
whole mile. It grew colder and colder as he climbed
higher and higher, and he stumbled upward in a fever of
confusion, sinking into snow up to his armpits. Suddenly,
when he thought he'd reached the limits of his powers of
endurance, he saw a pale shadow at the side of a precipice.
He collapsed before the door of the *Hospice*, paralyzed
with cold. When he managed with difficulty to ring the
bell, a snarling ugly young monk opened the door to him
and took him to a dirty little room and impatiently gave
him the usual meal: a bowl of soup, some bread and
cheese, a glass of wine. A hard mattress and flimsy blan-
ket were then given to him and in the middle of the
night, Rimbaud thought he could hear monks singing
hymns of joy at having once again robbed the various
governments that subsidized the place. The next morning,
after more bread and cheese, Rimbaud left, not much
rested. It was a fine day, the wind had died down, and the
mountains were illuminated by the brilliant Alpine sun-
light. There was no more climbing now, it was down-
mountain all the way. Down and down he jogged till he
came to warmer air. Then he saw vineyards and fields,
birds and farms and cows. At last he reached Lugano,
where he could get a train for Genoa on time to board
the boat for Alexandria. He was now no longer the angel-
faced boy-poet of 1872. At the age of twenty four, his

hair had turned gray and he wore a bleached frizzy little beard. He looked like a walking corpse — but still restlessly *seeking* something. *Le pélerin de l'absolu jusqu'à la fin, quoi!* Today tourists who visit the temple of Luxor, near Alexandria, are shown the name 'RIMBAUD' deeply carved in the stone high up on a pillar. Almost 100 years have gone by since someone carved that name there. No one knows to this day how it got there.

Bertrand Mathieu
New Haven, Connecticut

I
LIFE OF THE CHILD

*"We're in the months of love; I'm
seventeen years old. The time of hopes
and dreams, as they say — and here I
am, getting started — a child touched by
the finger of the Muse — excuse me if
that's trite — to express my fine beliefs,
my yearnings, my feelings, all those
things poets know — myself, I call them
spring things."*

Letter to Théodore de Banville
Charleville, May 1870.

APRÈS LE DÉLUGE

Aussitôt que l'idée du Déluge se fut rassise,
Un lièvre s'arrêta dans les sainfoins et les clochettes
mouvantes, et dit sa prière à l'arc-en-ciel à travers la
toile de l'araignée.

Oh! les pierres précieuses qui se cachaient, — les
fleurs qui regardaient déjà.

Dans la grande rue sale les étals se dressèrent, et l'on
tira les barques vers la mer étagée là-haut comme sur les
gravures.

Le sang coula, chez Barbe-Bleue, — aux abattoirs —
dans les cirques, où le sceau de Dieu blêmit les fenêtres.
Le sang et le lait coulèrent.

Les castors bâtirent. Les « mazagrans » fumèrent dans
les estaminets.

Dans la grande maison de vitres encore ruisselante,
les enfants en deuil regardèrent les merveilleuses images.

Une porte claqua, et sur la place du hameau, l'enfant
tourna ses bras, compris des girouettes et des coqs des
clochers de partout, sous l'éclatante giboulée.

Madame*** établit un piano dans les Alpes. La messe
et les premières communions se célébrèrent aux cent
mille autels de la cathédrale.

Les caravanes partirent. Et le Splendide-Hôtel fut bâti
dans le chaos de glaces et de nuit de pôle.

Depuis lors, la Lune entendit les chacals piaulant par
les déserts de thym, — et les églogues en sabots grogn-
ant dans le verger. Puis, dans la futaie violette, bour-
geonnante, Eucharis me dit que c'était le printemps.

AFTER THE FLOOD

Right after the idea of the Flood had simmered down,

A rabbit stood still in the clover and swinging flower-bells, and said a prayer to the rainbow through the spider's web.

Wow! the priceless stones that were hiding — the flowers that were regaining their eyesight.

In the messy main street, display cases were being built and boats were being dragged to the sea piled high like in etchings.

The blood flowed at Bluebeard's — through the stockyards — at the circuses, wherever God's touch turned the windows white. Both blood and milk flowed.

Beavers kept building. Coffee pots kept steaming up the insides of cafés.

In the big house with windowpanes still dripping, children in mourning were looking at the marvelous pictures.

A door crashed! and on the town parade ground, the boy waved his arms and was recognized right away by weathervanes and steeple cocks from all over in that crackling downpour.

Madam So-and-So set up a piano in the Alps. Mass and first communions were being celebrated at the hundred thousand altars of the cathedral.

Motorcades were setting out. And the Hotel Splendid was built in the chaos of ice and polar night.

Since then, the Moon has been hearing wild dogs howling in deserts of thyme — and eclogues in wooden shoes growling in the orchard. And now, in a budding grove crowded with violets, an Amazon lily tells me spring has come.

Sourds, étang. — Ecume, roule sur le pont et par-
desus les bois; — draps noirs et orgues, éclairs et
tonnerre, — montez et roulez; — Eaux et tristesses,
montez et relevez les Déluges.

Car depuis qu'ils se sont dissipés, — oh les pierres
précieuses s'enfouissant, et les fleurs ouvertes! — c'est
un ennui! et la Reine, la Sorcière qui allume sa braise
dans le pot de terre, ne voudra jamais nous raconter ce
qu'elle sait, et que nous ignorons.

Flood, pond! — Foam, pour over the bridge and all over the woods! Dark organs and shrouds, thunder and lightning, *rise high* and lay us out flat! — Waters and miseries, rise up and bring back more Floods.

Because since they disappeared — *aie!* the priceless stones being buried and the flowers out of sight! — it's been a bore! and the Queen, the Witch that lights her fire in an earthenware bowl, won't ever tell us what she knows, what we'll *never* know.

AUBE

J'ai embrassé l'aube d'été.

Rien ne bougeait encore au front des palais. L'eau
était morte. Les camps d'ombres ne quittaient pas la route
du bois. J'ai marché, réveillant les haleines vives et
tièdes, et les pierreries regardèrent, et les ailes se
levèrent sans bruit.

La première entreprise fut, dans le sentier déjà empli
de frais et blêmes éclats, une fleur qui me dit son nom.

Je ris au wasserfall blond qui *s'échevela* à travers les
sapins : à la cime argentée je reconnus la déesse.

Alors je levai un à un les voiles. Dans l'allée, en
agitant les bras. Par la plaine, où je l'ai dénoncée au coq.
A la grand'ville elle fuyait parmi les clochers et les
dômes, et courant comme un mendiant sur les quais de
marbre, je la chassais.

En haut de la route, près d'un bois de lauriers, je l'ai
entourée avec ses voiles amassés, et j'ai senti un peu son
immense corps. L'aube et l'enfant tombèrent au bas du
bois.

Au réveil il était midi.

DAWN

I've embraced the summer dawn.

Nothing budged yet on the walls of the palaces.
The water was dead still. Crowds of shadows squatted in
place on the road to the woods. I tramped on, waking up
the lukewarm living breezes, and the stones watched, and
wings were beating without sound.

The first real happening, on the little path already
filled with fresh pale flashings, was a flower that laid its
name on me.

I chuckled at the blond waterfall *disheveled* through
the pine trees: at their silvered tips, I spotted the god-
dess.

Quick I started lifting her veils, one by one. In the
path, by waving my arms. In the field, where I gave her
away to the cock. All over town, she *ran* between the
steeples and domes, and moving like a hustler on the
piers of marble, I hassled her!

Where the road turns upwards, near a laurel wood, I
bundled her all up in her veils, and I felt her huge body
a bit. Dawn and the child dropped together at the wood's
edge.

When I woke it was noon.

ENFANCE

I

Cette idole, yeux noirs et crin jaune, sans parents ni cour, plus noble que la fable, mexicaine et flamande; son domaine, azur et verdure insolents, court sur des plages nommées, par des vagues sans vaisseaux, de noms férocement grecs, slaves, celtiques.

A la lisière de la forêt, — les fleurs de rêve tintent, éclatent, éclairent, — la fille à lèvre d'orange, les genoux croisés dans le clair déluge qui sourd des prés, nudité qu'ombrent, traversent et habillent les arcs-en-ciel, la flore, la mer.

Dames qui tournoient sur les terrasses voisines de la mer; enfantes et géantes, superbes noires dans la mousse vert-de-gris, bijoux debout sur le sol gras des bosquets et des jardinets dégelés, — jeunes mères et grandes soeurs aux regards pleins de pèlerinages, sultanes, princesses de démarche et de costume tyranniques, petites étrangères et personnes doucement malheureuses.

Quel ennui, l'heure du « cher corps » et « cher coeur »!

CHILDHOOD

I

This fetish, eyes black and yellow mane, no family and no following, but placed higher up than Mexican or Flemish fairy tales; his turf, smart-alecky blue and green, extends to beaches which boatless waves have ferociously called Greek, Slavic, Celtic.

At the wood's edge — dream flowers buzz, flash, illuminate — the girl with the orange lips, knees crossed in the clear flood springing up from the fields, her nakedness shadowed, penetrated, dressed up by rainbows, flora, sea.

Ladies who're strolling on balconies next to the sea; baby girls and she-giants, superb black women in gray-green foam, jewels erect in the rich soil of groves and little thawed gardens — young mothers and big sisters with eyes brimful of pleasure-trips, sultanas, princesses tyrannical in their stride and their get-up, little foreign chicks and cuties mildly unhappy.

What a *bore,* the idea of "dear girl" and "dear heart."

II

C'est elle, la petite morte, derrière les rosiers. — La
jeune maman trépassée descend le perron. — La calèche
du cousin crie su le sable. — Le petit frère (il est aux
Indes!) là, devant le couchant, sur le pré d'oeillets. — Les
vieux qu'on a enterrés tout droits dans le rempart aux
giroflées.

L'essaim des feuilles d'or entoure la maison du général.
Ils sont dans le midi. — On suit la route rouge pour
arriver à l'auberge vide. Le château est à vendre; les
persiennes sont détachées. — Le curé aura emporté la clef
de l'église. — Autour de parc, les loges des gardes sont
inhabitées. Les palissades sont si hautes qu'on ne voit que
les cimes bruissantes. D'ailleurs, il n'y a rien à voir là-
dedans.

Les prés remontent aux hameaux sans coqs, sans
enclumes. L'écluse est levée. O les calvaires et les mou-
lins du désert, les îles et les meules!

Des fleurs magiques bourdonnaient. Les talus le
berçaient. Des bêtes d'une élégance fabuleuse circulaient.
Les nuées s'amassaient sur la haute mer faite d'une éter-
nité de chaudes larmes.

II

She's here, the little girl, dead behind the rosebushes. —
The young mother, dead also, walks down the steps. —
The cousin's carriage creaks in the sand. — The little
brother (he's in India!) right there, in front of the sunset,
in the field of carnations. — The old men they've buried
upright in the wall smothered with gillyflowers.

Swarms of gold leaves surround the general's house.
They're in the south. — You follow the red road to reach
the empty inn. The château's up for sale and the shutters
are falling apart. — The priest must have spirited away
the key to the church. — All over the grounds, the keep-
ers' cabins are empty. The fences are so high you can only
see the treetops blowing in the wind. Besides, there's
nothing to see in there.

The fields are crowding in on these towns with no
cocks and no anvils. The sluice gates are open. O the
crucifixions and the blow mills, O the islands and the
haystacks!

Magic flowers were buzzing out loud. The slopes were
rocking him. Fabulously gorgeous animals were making
the rounds. Clouds were gathering over high seas made up
of eternities of scalding tears.

III

Au bois il y a un oiseau, son chant vous arrête et vous fait rougir.

Il y a une horloge qui ne sonne pas.

Il y a une fondrière avec un nid de bêtes blanches.

Il y a une cathédrale qui descend et un lac qui monte.

Il y a une petite voiture abandonnée dans le taillis, ou qui descend le sentier en courant, enrubannée.

Il y a une troupe de petits comédiens en costumes, aperçus sur la route à travers la lisière du bois.

Il y a enfin, quand l'on a faim et soif, quelqu'un qui vous chasse.

IV

Je suis le saint, en prière sur la terrasse — comme les bêtes pacifiques paissent jusqu'à la mer de Palestine.

Je suis le savant au fauteuil sombre. Les branches et la pluie se jettent à la croisée de la bibliothèque.

Je suis le piéton de la grand'route par les bois nains; la rumeur des écluses couvre mes pas. Je vois longtemps la mélancolique lessive d'or du couchant.

Je serais bien l'enfant abandonné sur la jetée partie à la haute mer, le petit valet suivant l'allée dont le front touche le ciel.

Les sentiers sont âpres. Les monticules se couvrent de genêts. L'air est immobile. Que les oiseaux et les sources sont loin! Ce ne peut être que la fin du monde, en avançant.

III

In the woods there's a bird, his song stops you
dead and makes you blush.
   There's a clock that doesn't strike.
   There's a quagmire with a nest of white animals.
   There's a cathedral that goes down and a lake that
comes up.
   There's a little toy wagon ditched in the bushes or else,
zooming down the road, all covered with ribbons.
   There's a troupe of little actors in costumes, glimpsed
on the road at the woods' edge.
   And when you get hungry and thirsty, there's someone
there to hassle you.

IV

I'm the saint, saying prayers on the balcony — just
like the peace-loving animals that graze all the way to the
sea of Palestine.
   I'm the scholar in his dark easychair. The branches and
the rain beat against my library windows.
   I'm the hitchhiker on the highways that run through
low woods. The roar of the sluices drowns out my steps.
I look a long while at the depressing gold-smudged wash
of the setting sun.
   I could easily be the kid abandoned on a pier that's
heading out for the high seas, the farm boy following the
trail whose upper reaches touch the sky.
   The paths are rough. The knollsides are covered with
stubble. The air is motionless. How far-off are the birds
and the faucets! This has *got* to be the end of the world,
this moving *ahead*.

V

Qu'on me loue enfin ce tombeau, blanchi à la chaux avec les lignes du ciment en relief — très loin sous terre.

Je m'accoude à la table, la lampe éclaire très vivement ces journaux que je suis idiot de relire, ces livres sans intérêt. —

A une distance énorme au'dessus de mon salon souterrain, les maisons s'implantent, les brumes s'assemblent. La boue est rouge ou noire. Ville monstrueuse, nuit sans fin!

Moins haut, sont des égouts. Aux côtés, rien que l'épaisseur de globe. Peut-être des gouffres d'azur, des puits de feu. C'est peut-être sur ces plans que se rencontrent lunes et comètes, mers et fables.

Aux heures d'amertume je m'imagine des boules de saphir, de métal. Je suis maître du silence. Pourquoi une apparence de soupirail blémirait-elle au coin de la voûte?

V

Let them rent me this grave, insides whitewashed, with cement lines in relief — far down underground.

I lean my elbows on the table, the lamp shines brightly on these newspapers which I'm dumb enough to read again, these idiotic books.

At a tremendous distance over my underground living-room, the houses sink roots, the fogs gather round. The muck is red or black. NIGHTMARE CITY! Night without limits!

Less high up are the sewers. Around me, only the thickness of the globe. Perhaps abysses of azure or deep wells of fire. Or perhaps at these levels rendezvous occur between comets and moons, myths and seas.

When I'm *really* down, I imagine balls of sapphire, balls of metal. I'm master of this silence. So why should the outlines of a vent begin to *flash, faintly,* at the corner of my ceiling?

JEUNESSE

I
Dimanche

Les calculs de côté, l'inévitable descente du ciel et la
visite des souvenirs et la séance des rhythmes occupent la
demeure, la tête et le monde de l'esprit.
— Un cheval détale sur le turf suburbain et le long des
cultures et des boisements, percé par la peste carbonique.
Une misérable femme de drame, quelque part dans le
monde, soupire après des abandons improbables. Les
desperadoes languissent après l'orage, l'ivresse et les
blessures. De petits enfants étouffent des malédictions le
long des rivières. —
Reprenons l'étude au bruit de l'oeuvre dévorante qui
se rassemble et remonte dans les masses.

II
Sonnet

Homme de constitution ordinaire, la chair n'était-elle
pas un fruit pendu dans le verger, ô journées enfantes!
le corps un trésor à prodiguer; ô aimer, le péril ou la
force de Psyché? La terre avait des versants fertiles en
princes et en artistes, et la descendance et la race nous
poussaient aux crimes et aux deuils : le monde, votre
fortune et votre péril. Mais à présent, ce labeur comblé,
toi, tes calculs, toi, tes impatiences, ne sont plus que
votre danse et votre voix, non fixées et point forcées,
quoique d'un double événement d'invention et de succès
une raison, en l'humanité fraternelle et discrète par l'uni-
vers sans images; — la force et le droit réfléchissent la
danse et la voix à présent seulement appréciées . . .

YOUTH

I
Sunday

When schoolwork's set aside, the inevitable descent
from the blue yonder and the return of memories and
the stilling of rhythms become the concerns of family
life, the head, and "the realm of the spirit."
— A horse is scampering off on the suburban turf,
along the gardens and wood lots, nauseated by the car-
bonic plague. Somewhere in the world, a doomed thea-
trical woman is sighing for unlikely desertions. Despera-
dos are just dying for scraps, or drunkenness, or wounds.
Little children are choking on their own blasphemies
along the rivers.
Let's get back to studying in the midst of the thunder-
ing task that's regrouping and rising in the masses.

II
Sonnet

MAN of ordinary constitution, wasn't the flesh a fruit
hanging in the orchard? O days of the child — wasn't the
body a treasure to squander? O to love, the peril or power
of Psyche? The earth had slopes fertile with princes and
artists, and ancestry and race drove you to crimes and to
mourning: the world, your fortune and your danger. But
now that this work's completed, you, your schemings —
you, your impatiences — are merely your dance and your
voice, not fixed and not forced, although the reason for
the twofold achievement of invention and success is here:
in a mankind both separate and together, filling an image-
less universe — might and right both echoing your dance
and your voice, only *now* appreciated . . .

43

III
Vingt Ans

Les voix instructives exilées . . . L'ingénuité physique amèrement rassise . . . Adagio. Ah! l'égoïsme infini de l'adolescence, l'optimisme studieux : que le monde était plein de fleurs cet été! Les airs et les formes mourant . . . Un choeur, pour calmer l'impuissance et l'absence! Un choeur de verres, de mélodies nocturnes . . . En effet les nerfs vont vite chasser.

IV

Tu en es encore à la tentation d'Antoine. L'ébat du zèle écourté, les tics d'orgueil puéril, l'affaissement et l'effroi.

Mais tu te mettras à ce travail : toutes les possibilités harmoniques et architecturales s'émouvront autour de ton siège. Des êtres parfaits, imprévus, s'offriront à tes expériences. Dans tes environs affluera rêveusement la curiosité d'anciennes foules et de luxes oisifs. Ta mémoire et tes sens ne seront que la nourriture de ton impulsion créatrice. Quant au monde, quand tu sortiras, que sera-t-il devenu? En tout cas, rien des apparences actuelles.

III
Twenty Years Old

The teaching voices exiled . . . Physical candor bitterly
slapped down . . . Adagio. Ah! the limitless egotism of
adolescence, the studious optimism: how the world was
full of flowers that summer! Melodies and forms dying
out . . . A choir, to calm down impotence and absence! A
choir of glasses, of nighttime tunes . . . All right, the
nerves are always ready to run.

IV

You're still at St. Anthony's temptation. The bout with
diminished zeal, the tics of boyish pride, the collapse and
the terror.

But you're going to get to work: all harmonic and archi-
tectonic possibilities will surge around your seat. Perfect
beings, unimaginable, will offer themselves to you to
experiment with. All around you the curiosity of ancient
crowds and idle wealth will dreamily flow in. Your mem-
ory and your senses will merely serve to feed your crea-
tive impulses. As for the world, what's going to become
of it after you've gone? Anyway, not a *trace* of its current
appearances.

GUERRE

Enfant, certains ciels ont affiné mon optique : tous les caractères nuancèrent ma physionomie. Les Phénomènes s'émurent. — A présent, l'inflexion éternelle des moments et l'infini des mathématiques me chassent par ce monde où je subis tous les succès civils, respecté de l'enfance étrange et des affections énormes, — Je songe à une Guerre, de droit ou de force, de logique bien imprévue.

C'est aussi simple qu'une phrase musicale.

WAR

As a child, my eyesight was sharpened by certain skies:
their features deep-darkened my whole appearance. The
Phenomena came alive! — Right now, the endless inflec-
tions of temporality and the infinity of mathematics are
tracking me down all over this world in which I put up
with civic acclaim, famous among weird kids and crushing
displays of feeling. I dream of a War, of right or of might,
of unthinkable logic.

It's as simple as a musical phrase.

ANGOISSE

Se peut-il qu'Elle me fasse pardonner les ambitions continuellement écrasées, — qu'une fin aisée répare les âges d'indigence, — qu'un jour de succès nous endorme sur la honte de notre inhabileté fatale?

(O palmes! diamant! — Amour, force! — plus haut que toutes joies et gloires! — de toutes façons, partout, — démon, dieu, — Jeunesse de cet être-ci : moi!)

Que des accidents de féerie scientifique et des mouvements des fraternité sociale soient chéris comme restitution progressive de la franchise première? . . .

Mais la Vampire qui nous rend gentils commande que nous nous amusions avec ce qu'elle nous laisse, ou qu'autrement nous soyons plus drôles.

Rouler aux blessures, par l'air lassant et la mer; aux supplices, par le silence des eaux et de l'air meurtriers; aux tortures qui rient, dans leur silence atrocement houleux.

ANGUISH

Can it be that She'll have me acquitted for ambitions
consistently squelched? — that wealth in the end will
make up for years of privation? — that one day's success
will wipe out the memory of my fatal lack of skill?

(O palms! diamonds! — Love! strength! — greater than
all joys and all fame! — in every way — everywhere,
demon and god — Seedtime of this being: me!)

That the lucky streak of Modern Science and the move-
ment for Social Equality will be recognized as the right
roads back to our earliest freedom . . .?

But the Vampire that makes us behave orders us to
play with what she leaves us, or else grow up to be
freaks.

Wrapped up in my wounds, through the tiresome air
and the sea; in my torments, through the silence of waters
and cutthroat air; in tortures that laugh out loud, in their
crushing heaves of silence.

DÉMOCRATIE

« Le drapeau va au paysage immonde, et notre patois étouffe le tambour.

« Aux centres nous alimenterons la plus cynique prostitution. Nous massacrerons les révoltes logiques.

« Aux pays poivrés et détrempés! — au service des plus monstrueuses exploitations industrielles ou militaires.

« Au revoir ici, n'importe où. Conscrits du bon vouloir, nous aurons la philosophie féroce; ignorants pour la science, roués pour le confort; la crevaison pour le monde qui va. C'est la vraie marche. En avant, route! »

DEMOCRACY

"The flag's taking off for that filthy place, and our slogans are drowning out the drums.

"In the big cities, we'll keep alive an all-out cynical whoring. We'll massacre all revolts that make sense.

"On to the wasted and dried-up countries! — at the service of the most monstrously efficient military-industrial complexes. Goodbye to here, forget what's there. Recruits of good will, we'll have a terrific philosophy. Not caring for science, eager for comforts. Let the rest of the world go blow! This is the real thing. Forwa-a-a-a-a-a-ard, MARCH!"

H

Toutes les monstruosités violent les gestes atroces d'Hortense. Sa solitude est la mécanique érotique, sa lassitude, la dynamique amoureuse. Sous la surveillance d'une enfance elle a été, à des époques nombreuses, l'ardente hygiène des races. Sa porte est ouverte à la misère. Là, la moralité des êtres actuels se décorpore en sa passion ou en son action. — O terrible frisson des amours novices sur le sol sanglant et par l'hydrogène clarteux! trouvez Hortense.

H

All these monstrosities are ravishing Hortense's heart-
less dumb show. Her solitudes mean erotic mechanics;
her lassitude, love's dynamisms. On the proving ground
of childhood, she's often been the grabbed-at hygiene of
the races. Her door's wide open to impoverishment.
There, the morals of living beings are stripped of bodies
in her passion or her action. — O naughty shudderings of
novice love on the bleeding floor, in the transfigured
air! — locate Hortense.

II
LIFE OF THE POET

"The sufferings are enormous, but one has to be tough, one has to be born a poet, and I've come to realize I'm a poet. It's not at all my fault. It's wrong to say: I think. One has to say: I am thought . . . I is another. Too bad for the wood that finds itself a violin, and nuts to the unaware who babble and cackle about things they can't understand at all!"

Letter to Georges Izambard
(Charleville, May 1871).

CONTE

Un Prince était vexé de ne s'être employé jamais qu'à la perfection des générosités vulgaires. Il prévoyait d'étonnantes révolutions de l'amour, et soupçonnait ses femmes de pouvoir mieux que cette complaisance agrémentée de ciel et de luxe. Il voulait voir la vérité, l'heure du désir et de la satisfaction essentiels. Que ce fût ou non une aberration de piété, il voulut. Il possédait au moins un assez large pouvoir humain.

Toutes les femmes qui l'avaient connu furent assassinées. Quel saccage du jardin de la beauté! Sous le sabre, elles le bénirent. Il n'en commanda point de nouvelles.— Les femmes réapparurent.

Il tua tous ceux qui le suivaient, après la chasse ou les libations. — Tous le suivaient.

Il s'amusa à égorger les bêtes de luxe. Il fit flamber les palais. Il se ruait sur les gens et les taillait en pièces. — La foule, les toits d'or, les belles bêtes existaient encore.

Peut-on s'extasier dans la destruction, se rajeunir par la cruauté! Le peuple ne murmura pas. Personne n'offrit le concours de ses vues.

Un soir il galopait fièrement. Un Génie apparut, d'une beauté ineffable, inavouable même. De sa physionomie et de son maintien ressortait la promesse d'un amour multiple et complexe! d'un bonheur indicible, insupportable même! Le Prince et le Génie s'anéantirent probablement dans la santé essentielle. Comment n'auraient-ils pas pu en mourir? Ensemble donc ils moururent.

Mais ce Prince décéda, dans son palais, à un âge ordinaire. Le Prince était le Génie. Le Génie était le Prince.

La musique savante manque à notre désir.

TALE

A Prince was sick and tired of having wasted so much
of his time practicing the customary courtesies. He could
foresee dynamite revolutions of love and suspected his
women of being able to give much more than their com-
placencies, with a touch of Sunday morning and cockatoo.
He wanted to look at the truth, the hour of essential
desire and satisfaction! Even at the risk of overdoing
devotion. THAT's what he wanted! At least he had an
awfully large supply of mortal spunk.

All the women who had known him had to die: what
slaughter in the hen-house of beauty! They all blessed
him as the sword came down. He didn't order any new
ones. — All these chicks came back.

He killed all those who followed him, after hunting
or drinking bouts. — Everyone followed him.

He amused himself slitting the throats of really costly
beasts. He set fire to palaces. He would hurl himself on
people and hack them to pieces. — The crowds, the gol-
den rooftops, the beautiful beasts went on existing.

Can a person achieve true happiness through destruc-
tion? Can a man know rejuvenation through cruelty?
The people weren't complaining. No one offered the
benefit of his views.

One night he was horseback-riding, really cocky. A
Genie appeared, incredibly beautiful, un*speak*ably even.
His face and his bearing glowed with the promise of a
love both many-sided and complicated! of a happiness
indescribable, un*bear*able even! The Prince and the Genie
killed each other, most probably in essential health. How
could they help *dying* of it? Together then they died.

But this Prince died in his palace at the customary
age. The Prince was the Genie. The Genie was the Prince.
Our desires still lack a cunning music.

PARADE

Des drôles très solides. Plusieurs ont exploité vos
mondes. Sans besoins, et peu pressés de mettre en oeuvre
leurs brillantes facultés et leur expérience de vos con-
sciences. Quels hommes mûrs! Des yeux hébétés â la
façon de la nuit d'été, rouges et noirs, tricolores, d'acier
piqué d'étoiles d'or; des facies déformés, plombés, blêmis,
incendiés; des enrouements folâtres! La démarche cruelle
des oripeaux! — Il y a quelques jeunes, — comment
regarderaient-ils Chérubin? — pourvus de voix effra-
yantes et de quelques ressources dangereuses. On les
envoie prendre du dos en ville, affublés, d'un *luxe*
dégoûtant.

O le plus violent Paradis de la grimace enragée! Pas de
comparaison avec vos Fakirs et les autres bouffonneries
scéniques. Dans des costumes improvisés avec le goût du
mauvais rêve ils jouent des complaintes, des tragédies de
malandrins et de demi-dieux spirituels comme l'histoire
ou les religions ne l'ont jamais été. Chinois, Hottentots,
bohémiens, niais, hyènes, Molochs, vieilles démences,
démons sinistres, ils mêlent les tours populaires, mater-
nels, avec les poses et les tendresses bestiales. Ils inter-
préteraient des pièces nouvelles et des chansons « bonnes
filles ». Maîtres jongleurs, ils transforment le lieu et les
personnes et usent de la comédie magnétique. Les yeux
flambent, le sang chante, les os s'élargissent, les larmes et
des filets rouges ruissellent. Leur raillerie ou leur
terreur dure une minute, ou des mois entiers.

J'ai seul la clef de cette parade sauvage.

SIDE SHOW

Tough customers. Many of them took advantage of your
worlds. With no sweat at all, no hurry to make use of
their spectacular know-how and their understanding of
your tender consciences. Pretty virile men! Eyes listless
like a summer night, reddened and blackish, three-shaded,
steel studded with yellow stars. Faces twisted, leaden,
bloodless, gutted. Moronic hoarsenesses! The merciless
posturings of tinsel! — Some are young guys — what
would they think of Cherubino? — with bloodcurdling
voices and some pretty dangerous tricks. They send
these studs to town to bugger, decked out in *revolting*
duds.

O the specially violent Kingdom-Come of the raging
mouth! No comparison with your Fakirs and other stage
antics. In improvised costumes, with as much taste as bad
dreams, they act out sad songs and tragedies of thieves
and demigods more uplifting than history or religion have
ever managed to be! Chinese, Hottentots, gypsies, nitwits,
hyenas, Molochs, old lunacies, diabolical stunts, they mix
much-loved oldtime ditties meant for Mom with carni-
vorous winks and caresses. They're authorities on new
pieces for the stage and tunes about "fair lassies." Rugged
stuntsmen, they can transform both the scene and the
characters: they use magnetic tricks. The eyes glow, the
blood sings, the bones grow bigger, the tears and the
life-lines go traipsing. Their horseplay or their panic
terror may last a minute, or whole months.

I alone have the key to this screwy side show.

ANTIQUE

Gracieux fils de Pan! Autour de ton front couronné de
fleurettes et de baies, tes yeux, des boules précieuses,
remuent. Tachées de lies brunes, tes joues se creusent.
Tes crocs luisent. Ta poitrine ressemble à une cithare,
des tintements circulent dans tes bras blonds. Ton coeur
bat dans ce ventre où dort le double sexe. Promène-toi,
la nuit, en mouvant doucement cette cuisse, cette seconde
cuisse et cette jambe de gauche.

ANTIQUE

Gorgeous son of Pan! Beneath your brow crowned with flowers and berries, your eyes — these precious balls — look around. Streaked with coarse brown, your cheeks look hollow. Your fangs gleam. Your chest looks like a lyre, jingling sounds are moving down your blond arms. Your heart's beating in this belly where the double sex sleeps. Walk around, at night, and slowly move this thigh, then this other thigh and this left leg.

BOTTOM

La réalité étant trop épineuse pour mon grand carac-
tère, — je me trouvai néanmoins chez ma dame, en gros
oiseau gris bleu s'essorant vers les moulures du plafond
et traînant l'aile dans les ombres de la soirée.

Je fus, au pied de baldaquin supportant ses bijoux
adorés et ses chefs-d'oeuvre physiques, un gros ours aux
gencives violettes et au poil chenu de chagrin, les yeux
aux cristaux et aux argents des consoles.

Tout se fit ombre et aquarium ardent.

Au matin, — aube de juin batailleuse, — je courus
aux champs, âne, claironnant et brandissant mon grief,
jusqu'à ce que les Sabines de la banlieue vinrent se jeter
à mon poitrail.

BOTTOM

Reality being too prickly for my famous character — I
found myself nevertheless at my lady's in the shape of a
huge gray-blue bird soaring toward the moldings of the
ceiling and dragging my wings across the shadows of
the evening.

At the foot of the canopy supporting her adored jewels
and her physical masterpieces, I was a large bear with
purplish gums and a fur thick with misery, eyes of crystal
and silver from the consoles.

All things turned dark and ardent aquarium.

In the morning — aggressive dawn of June — I ran to
the fields, *ass*, braying and brandishing my grief, until
the Sabine women of the suburbs came and threw them-
selves at my torso.

BEING BEAUTEOUS

Devant une neige, un Être de Beauté de haute taille. Des sifflements de mort et des cercles de musique sourde font monter, s'élargir et trembler comme un spectre ce corps adoré; des blessures écarlates et noires éclatent dans les chairs superbes. Les couleurs propres de la vie se foncent, dansent, et se dégagent autour de la Vision, sur le chantier. Et les frissons s'élévent et grondent, et la saveur forcenée de ces effets se chargeant avec les sifflements mortels et les rauques musiques que le monde, loin derrière nous, lance sur notre mère de beauté, — elle recule, elle se dresse. Oh! nos os sont revêtus d'un nouveau corps amoureux.

O la face cendrée, l'écusson de crin, les bras de cristal! Le canon sur lequel je dois m'abattre à travers la mêlée des arbres et de l'air léger!

BEAUTIFUL BEING

Against some snow, a Beautiful Being exquisitely tall.
Whistlings of death and rings of unheard music make this
adored body grow taller, spring outward, and shiver like a
phantom: reddish and blackish wounds break open in the
superb flesh. — The colors of life itself deepen, dance
over, and drift around this Vision, on display to all
comers. Shiverings rise and rumble, and the frenetic
taste of these effects clashes with the mortal whistlings,
and the raucous music which the world, far beneath us,
hurls at our mother of beauty — she backs up, she rears
up. O our bones are all dressed up in newly turned-on
bodies!

O the face of ashes, the horsehair escutcheon, the
slippery limbs! the awesome leg-bone I've got to come
sliding down in this medley of trees and nimble breezes!

SCÈNES

L'ancienne Comédie poursuit ses accords et divise ses Idylles :

Des boulevards de tréteaux.

Un long pier en bois d'un bout à l'autre d'un champ rocailleux où la foule barbare évolue sous les arbres dépouillés.

Dans des corridors de gaze noire, suivant le pas des promeneurs aux lanternes et aux feuilles.

Des oiseaux comédiens s'abbattent sur un ponton de maçonnerie mû par l'archipel couvert des embaracations des spectateurs.

Des scènes lyriques accompagnées de flûte et de tambour s'inclinent dans des réduits ménagés sous les plafonds, autour des salons de clubs modernes ou des salles de l'Orient ancien.

La féerie manoeuvre au sommet d'un amphithéâtre couronné de taillis, — ou s'agite et module pour les Béotiens, dans l'ombre des futaies mouvantes sur l'arête des cultures.

L'opéra-comique se divise sur notre scène à l'arête d'intersection de dix cloisons dressées de la galerie aux feux.

SCENES

Ancient Comedy seeks its agreements and divides its
Idylls:

Boulevards to the stages.

A long wooden pier from one end of a rocky field to
another, where the untameable mob moves around under
the bare trees.

In hallways of black gauze, following in the footsteps
of the strollers among lanterns and leaves.

Birds out of mystery plays fly down to a concrete
pontoon moved by the covered archipelago of spectators
coming aboard.

Lyric scenes, accompanied by flute and drum, bend
down from narrowing corners around the ceilings of
modern clubs or halls of the ancient Orient.

The fairy-play is put on at the summit of an amphi-
theater crowned with thick shrubs — or noisily and
gently for the Boeotians in the shade of wind-blown
trees at the edge of the gardens.

The opéra-comique is broken up on a stage at the line
of intersection of ten partitions set up between the
gallery and the footlights.

VIES

I

O les énormes avenues du pays saint, les terrasses du temple! Qu'a-t-on fait de brahmane qui m'expliqua les Proverbes? D'alors, de là-bas, je vois encore même les vieilles! Je me souviens des heures d'argent et de soleil vers les fleuves, la main de la campagne sur mon épaule, et de nos caresses debout dans les plaines poivrées. — Un envol de pigeons écarlates tonne autour de ma pensée. — Exilé ici, j'ai eu une scène où jouer les chefs-d'oeuvre dramatiques de toutes les littératures. Je vous indiquerais les richesses inouïes. J'observe l'histoire des trésors que vous trouvâtes. Je vois la suite! Ma sagesse est aussi dédaignée que le chaos. Qu'est mon néant, auprés de la stupeur qui vous attend?

II

Je suis un inventeur bien autrement méritant que tous ceux qui m'ont précédé; un musicien même, qui ai trouvé quelque chose comme la clef de l'amour. A présent, gentilhomme d'une campagne aigre au ciel sobre, j'essaye de m'émouvoir au souvenir de l'enfance mendiante, de l'apprentissage ou de l'arrivée en sabots, des polémiques, des cinq ou six veuvages, et quelques noces où ma forte tête m'empêcha de monter au diapason des camarades. Je ne regrette pas ma vieille part de gaieté divine : l'air sobre de cette aigre campagne alimente fort activement mon atroce scepticisme. Mais comme ce scepticisme ne peut désormais être mis en oeuvre, et que d'ailleurs je suis dévoué à un trouble nouveau, — j'attends de devenir un très méchant fou.

LIVES

I

O the tremendous roadways of the holy country, the
temple terraces! What's become of the Brahmin who used
to teach me the Proverbs? I can still see even the old
women of that time, of that place! I remember hours full
of sunshine and silver near rivers, the touch of the
countryside on my shoulder, and our caresses as we stood
in the riddled fields. — A flight of blood-red pigeons
thunders over my thoughts. — In this exile of mine, I
used to have a stage where I could act out all the world's
dramatic literature. I could treat you to unperformed
masterpieces. I take in accounts of treasure *you* dis-
covered. I see what's coming! What I teach is looked
down on, like chaos. What's my nothingness compared to
the numbness that awaits YOU?

II

I'm an inventor far more deserving than the ones
who've turned up before my time; a musician who's
found something like the key of love, in fact. For the
time being I'm a blueblood from a bleak land in dark
times, trying to get high by remembering my hustling
childhood: learning the ropes, or getting there in wooden
shoes, or the hassles, or the five or six split-ups, or
several all-out gang-bangs when my level head saved me
from freaking out like my buddies. I don't regret my
share in those divine romps long ago: the bleak air of
that landscape's darkness actively nourishes my brutal
skepticism. But since this skepticism can't be played out
any time, and since I'm now being eaten alive by a new
torment — I expect to turn into a much madder scientist!

III

Dans un grenier où je fus enfermé à douze ans j'ai connu le monde, j'ai illustré la comédie humaine. Dans un cellier j'ai appris l'histoire. A quelque fête de nuit dans une cité de Nord, j'ai rencontré toutes les femmes des anciens peintres. Dans un vieux passage à Paris on m'a enseigné les sciences classiques. Dans une magnifique demeure cernée par l'Orient entier j'ai accompli mon immense oeuvre et passé mon illustre retraite. J'ai brassé mon sang. Mon devoir m'est remis. Il ne faut même plus songer à cela. Je suis réellement d'outre-tombe, et pas de commissions.

III

In an attic where I was locked up when I was twelve
I got acquainted with the world. I illustrated the human
comedy. In a wine cellar I studied history. At a night-
long carouse in a northern city, I bumped into the women
of all the old painters. In an old back-alley in Paris I was
taught the classical sciences. In a magnificent dwelling
surrounded by the entire Orient, I succeeded in my prodi-
gious Work and earned a well-deserved retirement. I
pushed my own blood. Now I'm off the hook. I mustn't
even think of that any more. I'm really six feet under,
so no special orders!

PHRASES

Quand le monde sera réduit en un seul bois noir pour nos quatre yeux étonnés, — en une plage pour deux enfants fidèles, — en une maison musicale pour notre claire sympathie, — je vous trouverai.

Qu'il n'y ait ici-bas qu'un vieillard seul, calme et beau, entouré d'un « luxe inouï », — et je suis à vos genoux.

Que j'aie réalisé tous vos souvenirs, — que je sois celle qui sait vous garrotter, — je vous étoufferai.

*

Quand nous sommes très forts, — qui recule? très gais, — qui tombe de ridicule? Quand nous sommes très méchants, — que ferait-on de nous?

Parez-vous, dansez, riez. Je ne pourrai jamais envoyer l'Amour par la fenêtre.

*

Ma camarade, mendiante, enfant monstre! comme ça t'est égal, ces malheureuses et ces manoeuvres, et mes embarras. Attache-toi à nous avec ta voix impossible, ta voix! unique flatteur de ce vil désespoir.

*

Une matinée couverte, en Juillet. Un goût de cendres vole dans l'air; — une odeur de bois suant dans l'âtre, — les fleurs rouies, — le saccage des promenades, — la bruine des canaux par les champs — pourquoi pas déjà les joujoux et l'encens?

*

SPELLS

When the world's nothing but one dark wood for our
four scared eyes — a beach for two crazy youngsters — a
musical house for our clear sympathy — I'll find you.
When there's only one old man left on earth, quiet and
beautiful, living among "unheard of luxuries" — I'll be at
your feet.
When I'm familiar with all your memories — when I'm
the girl who can bind your hands and feet — I'll *strangle*
you.

*

When we're very strong, who backs up? very happy,
who dies of shyness? When we're very bad, what can they
do to us?
Dress up, dance, laugh. I'll never want to toss Love out
the window.

*

My little buddy, hustler-girl, monstrous brat! You don't
even notice these miserable women and these sexy wiles
and my bashfulness. Hang on to us with your unbelievable
voice, your VOICE! sole admirer of this total despair.

*

Overcast morning, in July. A taste of ashes floats in the
air, the smell of sweaty wood in the fireplace, soaking
flowers, wastage all over the sidewalks, drizzle from the
canals above the fields — why not amusements right
NOW, and incense?

*

J'ai tendu des cordes de clocher à clocher; des guir-
landes de fenêtre à fenêtre; des chaînes d'or d'étoile à
étoile, et je danse.

*

Le haut étang fume continuellement. Quelle sorcière
va se dresser sur le couchant blanc? Quelles violettes
frondaisons vont descendre?

*

Pendant que les fond publics s'écoulent en fêtes de
fraternité, il sonne une cloche de feu rose dans les
nuages.

*

Avivant un agréable goût d'encre de Chine, une
poudre nôire pleut doucement sur ma veillée. — Je
baisse les feux du lustre, je me jette sur le lit, et, tourné
du côté de l'ombre, je vous vois mes filles, mes reines!

I've stretched some ropes from belfry to belfry, garlands from window to window, gold chains from star to star, and I dance.

*

The high pond is streaming endlessly. What witch will fly high over the white sunset? What purple foliage will come down?

*

While public moneys are being squandered on "fraternal banqueting," a bell of pink fire is ringing in the clouds.

*

Rekindling a pleasant taste for China ink, a black powder rains softly on my evening. I lower the jets of the chandelier, I throw myself on the bed and, turning my face toward the dark, *I see you*, my girls! my queens!

MATINÉE D'IVRESSE

O *mon* Bien! O *mon* Beau! Fanfare atroce où je ne trébuche point! Chevalet féerique! Hourra pour l'oeuvre inouïe et pour le corps merveilleux, pour la première fois! Cela commença sous les rires des enfants, cela finira par eux. Ce poison va rester dans toutes nos veines même quand, la fanfare tournant, nous serons rendus à l'ancienne inharmonie. O maintenant, nous si digne de ces tortures! rassemblons fervemment cette promesse surhumaine faite à notre corps et à notre âme créés : cette promesse, cette démence! L'élégance, la science, la la violence! On nous a promis d'enterrer dans l'ombre l'arbre du bien et du mal, de déporter les honnêtetés tyranniques, afin que nous amenions notre très pur amour. Cela commença par quelques dégoûts et cela finit, — ne pouvant nous saisir sur-le-champ de cette éternité — cela finit par une débandade de parfums.

Rire des enfants, discrétion des esclaves, austérité des vierges, horreur des figures et des objets d'ici, sacrés soyez-vous par le souvenir de cette veille. Cela commençait par toute la rustrerie, voici que cela finit par des anges de flamme et de glace.

Petite veille d'ivresse, sainte! quand ce ne serait que pour le masque dont tu nous as gratifié. Nous t'affirmons, méthode! Nous n'oublions, pas que tu as florifié hier chacun de nos âges. Nous avons foi au poison. Nous savons donner notre vie tout entière tous les jours.

Voici le temps des ASSASSINS.

TURNED-ON MORNING

My *kind* of Good! My *kind* of Beautiful! Mind-blowing jive that won't mess with my footwork! Cool torture, *far out!* Let's hear it for the good shit they can't hear and for the luscious body, this first time around! It's always *when kids die laughing* that these things start, and that's the way they'll *go*. It's a poison the blood gets hooked on, for good, even when your music's been zilched and you're into the old-time jazz again. So now that we're really digging this badass, let's come out and DEMAND action on that hyped-up promise they made our souls and bodies in their famous long ago: their promise, their mind-blow: Elegance, Violence, and Science! They were going to do some pruning on the tree of good and evil, *right?*, and put the screws to "freedom-loving" dictators: reduce pollution for lovers and freaks, *right?* It began just a bit disgusting and it ended — since we weren't quite quick enough to clinch our fabulous beat — it ended in a smell of *stampede.*

Kids that can laugh, slaves still up-tight, virgins now cooling it, faces and things made uglier by this place, keep in mind *we were free* for a spell, *we're all holy!* It started with outright trickery, but look how it's ending with angels of fire and ice!

Brief days being *high.* HOLY! if only because of the masks you taught us how to wear. *We accept you*, technique! We're flashing back to the brightness you gave to each of those days. The future's here — we trust in poison. We're going *the whole distance* from here on out.

Now's the time of the ASSASSINS.

VAGABONDS

Pitoyable frère! Que d'atroces veillées je lui dus! « Je ne me saisissais pas fervemment de cette entreprise. Je m'étais joué de son infirmité. Par ma faute nous retournerions en exil, en esclavage. » Il me supposait un guignon et une innocence très bizarres, et il ajoutait des raisons inquiétantes.

Je répondais en ricanant à ce satanique docteur, et finissais par gagner la fenêtre. Je créais, par delà la campagne traversée par des bandes de musique rare, les fantômes du futur luxe nocturne.

Après cette distraction vaguement hygiénique, je m'étendais sur une paillasse. Et, presque chaque nuit, aussitôt endormi, le pauvre frère se levait, la bouche pourrie, les yeux arrachés — tel qu'il se rêvait! — et me tirait dans la salle en hurlant son songe de chagrin idiot.

J'avais en effet, en toute sincérité d'esprit, pris l'engagement de le rendre à son état primitif de fils du Soleil, — et nous errions, nourris du vin des cavernes et du biscuit de la route, moi pressé de trouver le lieu et la formule.

VAGABONDS

Miserable brother! what terrible nights I owed him!
"I didn't put much passion into this affair. I simply
played on his weakness. It's my fault if we go back into
exile, into slavery." He figured I was jinxed and so
queerly innocent, and would add uneasy excuses.

I'd answer this satanic doctor with a jeer, and managed
to get to the window. I'd project, all over a landscape
filled with strips of odd music, phantasms of sensuous
nights to come.

After this vaguely hygenic distraction, I'd lie down on
a straw mat. And almost every night, as soon as I'd fall
asleep, the poor brother would get up, his mouth all dry
and his eyes bulging out — just as he dreamt he looked!
and would drag me into his room yowling his cock-eyed
dream of misery.

Id' made a vow, in absolute sincerity, to bring him
back again to his primitive state of son of the Sun —
and we drifted, kept alive by the wine of the subways and
the dry bread of the road, myself all on fire to find the
place and the formula.

III
LIFE IN NATURE

"The provinces, where people feed on flour
and mud, where they drink the local wine
and the local beer, that's not what I miss.
You're quite right to go on putting them
down. But this place: distillation, composi-
tion, all narrowness: and the suffocating
summer: the heat's not constant, but seeing
that fine weather is in everyone's interest
and that everyone is a pig, I hate summer
which kills me even when it appears a
little while. I'm as thirsty as a man with
gangrene: the Belgian and Ardennes rivers
and caves, THAT's what I miss."

Letter to Ernest Delahaye
(Paris, June 1872).

NOCTURNE VULGAIRE

Un souffle ouvre des brèches opéradiques dans les cloisons, — brouille le pivotement des toits rongés, — disperse les limites des foyers, — éclipse les croisées. —

Le long de la vigne, m'étant appuyé du pied à une gargouille, — je suis descendu dans ce carrosse dont l'époque est assez indiquée par les glaces convexes, les panneaux bombés et les sophas contournés. Corbillard de mon sommeil, isolé, maison de berger de ma niaiserie, le véhicule vire sur le gazon de la grande route effacée : et dans un défaut en haut de la glace de droite tournoient les blêmes figures lunaires, feuilles, seins!

— Un vert et un bleu très foncés envahissent l'image. Dételage aux environs d'une tache de gravier.

— Ici va-t-on siffler pour l'orage, et les Sodomes et les Solymes, et les bêtes féroces et les armées.

— (Postillon et bêtes de songe reprendront-ils sous les plus suffocantes futaies, pour m'enfoncer jusqu'aux yeux dans la source de soie)

— Et nous envoyer, fouettés à travers les eaux clapotantes et les boissons répandues, rouler sur l'aboi des dogues . . .

— Un souffle disperse les limites du foyer.

EVERYDAY NOCTURNE

A mere breath makes operatic cracks in the partitions — blurs the gyrations of the termite-eaten roofs — scatters the fireplace walls — wipes out the windows. —

After firmly steadying a foot on a gargoyle, I climbed down the vines to this coach the era of which is clearly enough indicated by its convex windowpanes, its bulging sides, and its contorted seats. Hearse of my sleep, by itself, shepherd's hut of my silliness, the vehicle turns around on the grass of the vanished highway: and in a defect in the top right-hand windowpane, deathly moon figures, leaves, and tits spin around!

— A very deep green and blue invade the picture. Unhitching in the vicinity of a bit of gravel.

— Here we'll whistle for the storm, for Sodoms and Solymas, and for wild beasts and armies.

— (Will the conductor and dream animals in the suffocating woods start all over and plunge me up to my eyes in the fountain of silk?)

— And send us, whipped by swishing waters and spilled drinks, rolling on the backs of yawping bulldogs . . .

— A mere breath *scatters* the fireplace walls.

FLEURS

D'un gradin d'or, — parmi les cordons de soie, les gazes grises, les velours verts et les disques de cristal qui noircissent comme du bronze au soleil, — je vois la digitale s'ouvrir sur un tapis de filigranes d'argent, d'yeux et de chevelures.

Des pièces d'or jaune semées sur l'agate, des piliers d'acajou supportant un dôme d'émeraudes, des bouquets de satin blanc et de fines verges de rubis entourent la rose d'eau.

Tels qu'un dieu aux énormes yeux bleus et aux formes de neige, la mer et le ciel attirent aux terrasses de marbre la foule des jeunes et fortes roses.

FLOWERS

From a gold step — among silk cords, gray gauzes, green velvets, and crystal discs that blacken like bronze in the sun — I see the foxglove opening up on a tapestry of silver filigree, and eyes, and heads of hair.

Coins of bright gold scattered on agate, mahogany columns supporting a dome of emeralds, bouquets of white satin and delicate inlays of rubies surround the waterrose.

Like a god with huge blue eyes and limbs like blizzards, the sky and sea entice to the marble stairway whole mobs of brash young roses.

MARINE

Les chars d'argent et de cuivre —
Les proues d'acier et d'argent —
Battent l'écume, —
Soulèvent les souches des ronces.
Les courants de la lande,
Et les ornières immenses du reflux,
Filent circulairement vers l'est,
Vers les piliers de la forêt,
Vers les fûts de la jettée,
Dont l'angle est heurté par des tourbillons de lumière.

SEASCAPE

Machines of silver and copper —
Prows of steel and silver —
Threshing the foam —
Turning over stumps of bramble.
The currents of the dunes —
The immense ruts of the ebb tide
Flowing circularly toward the East —
Toward the pylons of the forest —
Toward the timbers of the pier
Against whose boards whirlpools of daylight blow!

FÊTE D'HIVER

La cascade sonne derrière les huttes d'opéra-comique.
Des girandoles prolongent, dans les vergers et les allées
voisins du Méandre, — les verts et les rouges du cou-
chant. Nymphes d'Horace coiffées au Premier Empire, —
Rondes Sibériennes, Chinoises de Boucher.

WINTER CELEBRATION

The waterfall makes a noise behind the boxes of the opéra-comique. Candelabra extend into the orchards and alleyways near the Meander River — the greens and reds of the setting sun. Horatian nymphs in First Empire headdress — Siberian rondos and Boucher's Chinese ladies.

FAIRY

Pour Hélène se conjurèrent les sèves ornementales dans les ombres vierges et les clartés impassibles dans le silence astral. L'ardeur de l'été fut confiée à des oiseaux muets et l'indolence requise à une barque de deuils sans prix par des anses d'amours morts et de parfums affaissés.

— Après le moment de l'air des bûcheronnes à la rumeur du torrent sous la ruine des bois, de la sonnerie des bestiaux à l'écho des vals, et des cris des steppes. —

Pour l'enfance d'Hélène frissonnèrent les fourrures et les ombres — et le sein des pauvres, et les légendes du ciel.

Et ses yeux et sa danse supérieurs encore aux éclats précieux, aux influences froides, au plaisir du décor et de l'heure uniques.

FAIRYLAND

For Helen ornamental sap conspired in astral silence in the virginal darks and the impassive lights. The heat of summer was entrusted to speechless birds and a degree of laziness to a priceless mourning barge drifting through gulfs of dead loves and exhausted perfumes.

— After the time when the woodcutters' wives sang to the sound of the stream in the ruins of the woods, the time when the bells of the flocks rang out on the hills, and the cries of the steppes. —

For Helen's childhood the furs and shadows shivered — and the hearts of the poor, and the legends of heaven.

And her eyes and her dancing even better than the precious glitter, than the cold influence, than the pleasure of the perfect setting and the perfect moment.

IV
CITY LIFE

*"I want to work in freedom: but in Paris
which I love. Look here, I'm a pedestrian,
nothing more; I arrive in the immense city
without material resources: but you said to
me: Whoever wants to be a worker for fif-
teen cents a day applies here, does this,
lives like that. I apply here, do this, live
like that. I begged you to point out jobs
that aren't too involving because thinking
takes up large blocks of time. Releasing the
poet, these material seesaws become too
agreeable. I'm in Paris: I need a POSI-
TIVE ECONOMY!"*

Letter to Paul Demeny
(Charleville, August 1871).

OUVRIERS

O cette chaude matinée de février! Le Sud inopportun vint relever nos souvenirs d'indigents absurdes, notre jeune misère.

Henrika avait une jupe de coton à carreau blanc et brun, qui a dû être portée au siècle dernier, un bonnet à rubans, et un foulard de soie. C'était bien plus triste qu'un deuil. Nous faisions un tour dans la banlieue. Le temps était couvert, et ce vent du Sud excitait toutes les vilaines odeurs des jardins ravagés et des prés desséchés.

Cela ne devait pas fatiguer ma femme au même point que moi. Dans une flache laissée par l'inondation du mois précédent à un sentier assez haut, elle me fit remarquer de très petits poissons.

La ville, avec sa fumée et ses bruits de métiers, nous suivait très loin dans les chemins. O l'autre monde l'habitation bénie par le ciel et les ombrages! Le Sud me rappelait les misérables incidents de mon enfance, mes désespoirs d'été, l'horrible quantité de force et de science que le sort a toujours éloignée de moi. Non! nous ne passerons pas l'été dans cet avare pays où nous ne serons jamais que des orphelins fiancés. Je veux que ce bras durci ne traîne plus une *chère image!*

WORKERS

O that warm February morning! The unbothersome South came up here to agitate our ridiculous proletarian memories, our youthful poverty.

Henrika had on a brown and white checkered cotton skirt which must have been worn a hundred years ago, a bonnet with ribbons, a silk scarf. It was sadder than a wake. We were taking a walk in the suburbs. The day was overcast, and that wind from the South brought out all the bad smells from the dried-up fields and the gardens gone to pot.

This didn't manage to get my wife as tired as me. In a puddle left by the rains of the previous month on quite a high path, she showed me some very little fishes.

The city, with its smoke and its factory noises, followed us along the roads pretty far out. O that *other* world, that dwelling place bright with the sky above and shady spots! The South brought back those miserable memories of childhood, my summertime despairs, the horrible amounts of strength and knowledge fate has always robbed me of. No! we won't spend the summer in this avaricious place where we'll never be anything but a couple of love-sick castaways. I want this toughened arm of mine to quit lugging around a *pretty picture!*

LES PONTS

Des ciels gris de cristal. Un bizarre dessin de ponts, ceux-ci droits, ceux-là bombés, d'autres descendant ou obliquant en angles sur les premiers; et ces figures se renouvelant dans les autres circuits éclairés du canal, mais tous tellement longs et légers que les rives, chargées de dômes, s'abaissent et s'amoindrissent. Quelques-uns de ces ponts sont encore chargés de masures. D'autres soutiennent des mâts, des signaux, de frêles parapets. Des accords mineurs se croisent et filent; des cordes montent des berges. On distingue une veste rouge, peut-être d'autres costumes et des instruments de musique. Sont-ce des airs populaires, des bouts de concerts seigneuriaux, des restants d'hymnes publics? L'eau est grise et bleue, large comme un bras de mer.

Un rayon blanc, tombant du haut du ciel, anéantit cette comédie.

BRIDGES

Skies of gray crystal. A weird design of bridges, some straight, some arched, others coming down at oblique angles to the first; and these shapes repeating themselves in other lighted circles of the canal, but all so long and lightweight that the banks, loaded with domes, sink down and shrink. Several of these bridges are still covered with hovels. Others support masts, signals, frail ramparts. The lesser cables criss-cross each other and disappear; ropes rise from the shores. You can see a red jacket, possibly other costumes and musical instruments. Are these scraps of folk songs, odds and ends from highflown concerts, leftover public hymns? The water is gray, blue, broad as an arm of the sea.

A white ray, falling from high in the sky, squelches this silly scene.

VILLE

Je suis un éphémère et point trop mécontent citoyen
d'une métropole crue moderne parce que tout goût connu
a été éludé dans les ameublements et l'extérieur des
maisons aussi bien que dans le plan de la ville. Ici vous
ne signaleriez les traces d'aucun monument de supersti-
tion. La morale et la langue sont réduites à leur plus
simple expression, enfin! Ces millions de gens qui n'ont
pas besoin de se connaître amènent si pareillement
l'éducation, le métier et la vieillesse, que ce cours de vie
doit être plusieurs fois moins long que ce qu'une statis-
tique folle trouve pour les peuples de continent. Aussi
comme, de ma fenêtre, je vois des spectres nouveaux
roulant à travers l'épaisse et éternelle fumée de char-
bon, — notre ombre des bois, notre nuit d'été! — des
Erinnyes nouvelles, devant mon cottage qui est ma patrie
et tout mon coeur puisque tout ici ressemble à ceci, — la
Mort sans pleurs, notre active fille et servante, un Amour
désespéré et un joli Crime piaulant dans la boue de la rue.

CITY

I'm a temporary and not too discontented citizen of a metropolis that's obviously modern because all known standards of taste have been side-stepped in the furnishings and outsides of the houses as well as in the layout of the city. You'd have a hard time finding the least sign of any monument to superstition here. Morality and language have been reduced to their simplest expression, in short. These millions of citizens who haven't the slightest need to know each other conduct their education, their affairs, and their old age so completely alike that the better statisticians agree their life spans can only be several times less long than those of people on the Continent. Likewise, from my window, I watch new ghosts rolling through the thick everlasting coal smoke — our woodsy shade! our summer night! — the new Eumenides in front of my cottage which is my country and my whole heart since everything here looks like this — Death without tears, our competent girl and servant, a desperate Love, and a pretty Crime whining in the muck of the street.

ORNÌERES

A droite l'aube d'été éveille les feuilles et les vapeurs et les bruits de ce coin de parc, et les talus de gauche tiennent dans leur ombre violette les mille rapides ornières de la route humide. Défilé de féeries. En effet : des chars chargés d'animaux de bois doré, de mâts et de toiles bariolées, au grand galop de vingt chevaux de cirque tachetés, et les enfants et les hommes, sur leurs bêtes les plus étonnantes; — vingt véhicules, bossés, pavoisés et fleuris comme des carrosses anciens ou de contes, pleins d'enfants attifés pour une pastorale suburbaine. — Même des cercueils sous leur dais de nuit dressant les panaches d'ébène, filant au trot des grandes juments bleues et noires.

GROOVES

To the right the summer dawn wakes up the leaves and the mists and the sounds in this section of the park, and to the left the slopes contain in their purplish shade the thousand swift grooves of the sloshy road. Escapees from Happy Land! Here they come: floats loaded with golden wooden animals, poles and bright-painted posters vibrating to the frenzied gallop of twenty dappled circus horses, and children, and men, on their most fantastic beasts — twenty embossed wagons decorated with flags and flowers like ancient fairy tale coaches, full of children decked out for an outing in the suburbs. — Even coffins under pitch-dark canopies with jet-black plumes, zooming along to the trot of huge mares, all black and blue.

VILLES I

Ce sont des villes! C'est un peuple pour qui se sont montés ces Alleghanys et ces Libans de rêve! Des chalets de cristal et de bois qui se meuvent sur des rails et des poulies invisibles. Les vieux cratères ceints de colosses et de palmiers de cuivre rugissent mélodieusement dans les feux. Des fêtes amoureuses sonnent sur les canaux pendus derrière les chalets. La chasse des carillons crie dans les gorges. Des corporations de chanteurs géants accourent dans des vêtements et des oriflammes éclatants comme la lumière des cimes. Sur les plates-formes au milieu des gouffres les Rolands sonnent leur bravoure. Sur les passerelles de l'abîme et les toits des auberges l'ardeur du ciel pavoise les mâts. L'écroulement des apothéoses rejoint les champs des hauteurs où les centauresses séraphiques évoluent parmi les avalanches. Au-dessus du niveau des plus hautes crêtes une mer troublée par la naissance éternelle de Vénus, chargée de flottes orphéoniques et de la rumeur des perles et des conques précieuses, — la mer s'assombrit parfois avec des éclats mortels. Sur les versants des moissons de fleurs grandes comme nos armes et nos coupes, mugissent. Des cortèges de Mabs en robes rousses, opalines, montent des ravines. Là-haut, les pieds dans la cascade et les ronces, les cerfs tettent Diane. Les Bacchantes des banlieues sanglotent et la lune brûle et hurle. Vénus entre dans les cavernes des forgerons et des ermites. Des groupes de beffrois chantent les idées des peuples. Des châteaux bâtis en os sort la musique inconnue. Toutes les légendes évoluent et les élans se ruent dans les bourgs. Le paradis des orages s'effondre. Les sauvages dansent sans cesse la fête de la nuit. Et, une heure, je suis descendu dans le mouvement d'un boulevard de Bagdad où des compagnies ont chanté

CITIES I

These are *cities!* This is a *people* that these dream
Alleghenies and these dream Lebanons have sprung up
for! Bungalows of crystal and wood moving along invisi-
ble rails and pulleys. Old craters circled by colossi and
copper palm trees roaring with melody among the fires.
Love feasts ringing out on the suspended canals behind
the bungalows. The sounds of chimes chasing each other
in the gulleys. Guilds of gigantic singers coming together
in robes and banners as shining as the light on moutain
peaks. On scaffoldings among the abysses, Rolands roaring
with bravado. On foot-bridges over the depths and roofs
of inns, the brightness of the sky decking out the flag-
poles. The breakdown of apotheoses linking the fields
with the heights where seraphic she-centaurs ripen among
the avalanches. Above the level of the highest crests, a sea
stirred up by the ceaseless birth of Venus, brimming with
orphic navies and the roar of pearls and precious shells,
the sea at times grows dark with dying flashes. On the
slopes, harvests of flowers as big as our goblets and weap-
ons, howling. Long lines of Mabs in dresses of red and
opal climb up the ravines. Further up, standing in water-
falls and blackberries, stags suck Diana's tits. The Bac-
chantes of the suburbs sob, and the moon fumes and
hoots. Venus walks into the diggings of blacksmiths and
hermits. Crowds of bell towers ring out the ideas of the
people. An unfamiliar music flows out of castles built of
bones. All the legends come to a head and all the urges
hit the towns. The heaven of rages breaks down. The
savages dance non-stop the feast of night. And for a whole
hour, I went down into the noisy give-and-take of a boule-
vard in Bagdad where throngs of companions were joy-

la joie du travail nouveau, sous une brise épaisse, circulant sans pouvoir éluder les fabuleux fantômes des monts où l'on a dû se retrouver.

Quels bons bras, quelle belle heure me rendront cette région d'où viennent mes sommeils et mes moindres mouvements?

fully celebrating the New Work, in that breezy obscurity, moving ahead but not managing to steer clear of the fabulous phantasms of the mountains, where all had to orient themselves once again.

What strong arms? what beautiful hour? will give me back that region from which my sleep and my slightest moves derive.

VILLES II

L'acropole officielle outre les conceptions de la
barbarie moderne les plus colossales. Impossible d'ex-
primer le jour mat produit par ce ciel immuablement
gris, l'élat impérial des bâtisses, et la neige éternelle du
sol. On a reproduit dans un goût d'énormité singulier
toutes les merveilles classiques de l'architecture. J'assiste
à des expositions de peinture dans des locaux vingt fois
plus vastes qu'Hampton-Court. Quelle peinture! Un
Nabuchodonosor norwégien a fait construire les escaliers
des ministères; les subalternes que j'ai pu voir sont déjà
plus fiers que des Brahmanes, et j'ai tremblé à l'aspect des
gardiens de colosses et officiers de constructions. Par le
groupement des bâtiments en squares, cours et terrasses
fermées, on a évincé les cochers. Les parcs représentent
la nature primitive travaillée par un art superbe. Le haut
quartier a des parties inexplicables : un bras de mer, sans
bateaux, roule sa nappe de grésil bleu entre des quais
chargés de candélabres géants. Un pont court conduit à
une poterne immédiatement sous le dôme de la Sainte-
Chapelle. Ce dôme est une armature d'acier artistique de
quinze mille pieds de diamètre environ.

Sur quelques points des passerelles de cuivre, des
plates-formes, des escaliers qui contournent les halles et
les piliers, j'ai cru pouvoir juger la profondeur de la
ville! C'est le prodige dont je n'ai pu me rendre compte :
quels sont les niveaux des autres quartiers sur ou sous
l'acropole? Pour l'étranger de notre temps la reconnais-
sance est impossible. Le quartier commerçant est un circus
d'un seul style, avec galeries à arcades. On ne voit pas
de boutiques, mais la neige de la chaussée est écrasée;
quelques nababs aussi rares que les promeneurs d'un
matin de dimanche à Londres, se dirigent vers une dili-
gence de diamants. Quelques divans de velours rouge : on

CITIES II

The official acropolis outdistances the most colossal conceptions of modern barbarism. Impossible to do justice to the flat daylight produced by this immutably gray sky, the imperial glossiness of the buildings, and the eternal snow on the ground. With a unique taste for the gigantic, they have reproduced all the classical marvels of architecture, and I visit art exhibits in rooms twenty times the size of Hampton Court. What paintings! A Norwegian Nebuchadnezzar built the stairways of the government buildings; the second-stringers I met were already haughtier than the Big Shits, and I literally quaked at the sight of the guards of colossi and superintendents of structures. By grouping the buildings in squares, with yards and driveways closed, they're keeping out the cabs. The parks are displays of primitive nature improved with superb artistry, the upper part of town contains things no one can explain: an arm of the sea, with no boats, rolls up its sleet-blue sleeves between piers loaded with gigantic candelabra. A short bridge takes you to the back door right under the dome of the Sainte-Chapelle. This dome is an artistic framework of steel fifteen thousand feet in diameter, roughly.

From certain points on the copper footbridges, on the platforms, on the stairways that spiral up around the markets and the pillars, I thought I might be able to form an estimate of the city's depth! This is the marvel I couldn't figure out: What are the levels of the other districts above or beneath the acropolis? For the outsider of our time, recognition's impossible. The business district is a circus built in uniform style, with arcades added. The stores can't be seen, but the snow on the sidewalks is trampled: a few nabobs, as rare as walkers in London on a Sunday morning, are moving toward a diamond stagecoach. A few red velvet divans: ice-cold

sert des boissons polaires dont le prix varie de huit cents
à huit mille roupies. A l'idée de chercher des théâtres sur
ce circus, je me réponds que les boutiques doivent
contenir des drames assez sombres? Je pense qu'il y a une
police. Mais la loi doit être tellement étrange, que je
renonce à me faire une idée des aventuriers d'ici.

Le faubourg, aussi élégant qu'une belle rue de Paris,
est favorisé d'un air de lumière. L'élément démocratique
compte quelques cents âmes. Là encore, les maisons ne se
suivent pas; le faubourg se perd bizarrement dans la
campagne, le « Comté » qui remplit l'occident éternel
des forêts et des plantations prodigieuses où les gentils-
hommes sauvages chassent leurs chroniques sous la
lumière qu'on a créée.

drinks are served, varying in price from eight hundred to eight thousand rupees. When it occurs to me to look for theaters in this circus, I'm reminded that the stores must be featuring gloomy enough shows. I imagine there's a police force; but the law must be so weird that I give up trying to figure out what adventurers would *look* like here.

In the suburb, as beautiful as an elegant Paris street, the air you breathe is just like light, and the local democratic party numbers a few hundred souls. Here, also, the houses don't follow one another. The suburb loses itself strangely in the country, the "County," filling the everlasting west and the fantastic plantations where savage gentlemen track down their daily news by a light they've invented.

MÉTROPOLITAIN

Du détroit d'indigo aux mers d'Ossian, sur le sable rose et orange qu'a lavé le ciel vineux, viennent de monter et de se croiser des boulevards de cristal habités incontinent par de jeunes familles pauvres qui s'alimentent chez les fruitiers. Rien de riche. — La ville!

Du désert de bitume fuient droit en déroute avec les nappes de brumes échelonnées en bandes affreuses au ciel qui se recourbe, se recule et descend, formé de la plus sinistre fumée noire que puisse faire l'Océan en deuil, les casques, les roues, les barques, les croupes. — La bataille!

Lève le tête : ce pont de bois, arqué; les derniers potagers de Samarie; ces masques enluminés sous la lanterne fouettée par la nuit froide; l'ondine niaise à la robe bruyante, au bas de la rivière; les crânes lumineux dans les plants de pois — et les autres fantasmagories — la campagne.

Des routes bordées de grilles et de murs contenant à peine leurs bosquets, et les atroces fleurs qu'on appellerait coeurs et soeurs, Damas damnant de langueur, — possessions de féeriques aristocraties ultra-Rhénanes, Japonaises, Guaranies, propres encore à recevoir la musique des anciens — et il y a des auberges qui pour toujours n'ouvrent déjà plus — il y a des princesses, et, si tu n'es pas trop accablé, l'étude des astres — le ciel.

Le matin où avec Elle, vous vous débattîtes parmi les éclats de neige, les lèvres vertes, les glaces, les drapeaux noirs et les rayons bleus, et les parfums pourpres du soleil des pôles, — ta force.

METROPOLITAN

From the blue channels to Ossian's seas, over the pink
and orange sand washed by the winy sky, crystal boule-
vards have just risen and crossed, settled right away by
poor young families who get their groceries at the fruit-
stands. Nothing expensive. — The city, that's all!

From the asphalt desert, helmets, wheels, barges,
buttocks, run at break-neck speed with sheets of fog
spread out in atrocious strips across a sky that bends
back, pulls out, and comes down, shaped by the most
frightening black smoke the Ocean in mourning can
muster. — The battle, that's all!

Look up: this wooden bridge, arched; these last vege-
table gardens from Samaria; these illuminated masks
under the lantern whipped by the cold night; the silly
water nymph in a noisy dress, down by the river; these
luminous skulls in a row of peas — and the other im-
probabilities — The country, that's all.

Roads bordered by grillwork and walls that can barely
hold back their woods, and the terrible flowers called
hearts and sisters. Damask cursing quietly — possessions
of magic aristocracies. Upper-Rhenish, Japanese, Guaran-
ian, still qualified to intercept the music of the ancients —
and there are inns that now will never open again —
there are princesses and if you're not too overwhelmed,
the study of the stars. — The sky, that's all.

In the morning when you fought it out with Her among
these flashing snows, these icebergs, these black flags
and blue beams, and these purple perfumes of the polar
sun. — Your strength, that's all.

BARBARE

Bien après les jours et les saisons, et les êtres et les pays,

Le pavillon en viande saignante sur la soie des mers et des fleurs arctiques. (Elles n'existent pas.)

Remis des vieilles fanfares d'héroïsme — qui nous attaquent encore le coeur et la tête — loin des anciens assassins.

Oh! le pavillon en viande saignante sur la soie des mers et des fleurs arctiques. (Elles n'existent pas.)

Douceurs!

Les brasiers, pleuvant aux rafales de givre. — Douceurs! — les feux à la pluie du vent de diamants jetée par le coeur terrestre éternellement carbonisé pour nous. — O monde! —

(Loin des vieilles retraites et des vieilles flammes qu'on entend, qu'on sent.)

Les brasiers et les écumes. La musique, virement des gouffres et choc des glaçons aux astres.

O Douceurs, ô monde, ô musique! Et là, les formes, les sueurs, les chevelures et les yeux, flottant. Et les larmes blanches, bouillantes, — ô douceurs! — et la voix féminine arrivée au fond des volcans et des grottes arctiques.

Le pavillon . . .

BARBARIAN

Long after the days and the seasons, the people and
countries,
The flag of bleeding meat on the silk of seas and artic
flowers; (they don't exist).
Recovered from the old fanfares of heroism — which
still assault our hearts and heads — far from the old-time
assassins.
— O the flag of bleeding meat on the silk of seas and
arctic flowers; (they don't exist).
Pleasures!
Live embers, raining down in frosted gusts — Plea-
sures! — fires in a rain of diamond-filled wind flung out
by the earth's heart everlastingly carbonized for us. —
O world! —
(Far from the old hideaways and the old flames we can
hear, can feel.)
Fires and foam. Music, whirling of abysses and clacking
of icicles against the stars.
O pleasures, o world, o music! And here, the forms,
the sweating, the long hair and the eyes, floating. And
the white tears, burning — o pleasures! — and the female
voice reaching to the depths of volcanoes and arctic
dugouts.
The flag . . .

PROMONTOIRE

L'aube d'or et la soirée frissonnante trouvent notre
brick en large en face de cette villa et de ses dépendances,
qui forment un promontoire aussi étendu que l'Épire et
le Péloponnèse, ou que la grande île du Japon, ou que
l'Arabie! Des fanums qu'éclaire la rentrée des théories,
d'immenses vues de la défense des côtes modernes; des
dunes illustrées de chaudes fleurs et de bacchanales; de
grands canaux de Carthage et des Embankments d'une
Venise louche; de molles éruptions d'Etnas et des
crevasses de fleurs et d'eaux des glaciers; des lavoirs
entourés de peupliers d'Allemagne; des talus de parcs
singuliers penchant des têtes d'Arbre du Japon; et les
façades circulaires des « Royal » ou des « Grand » de
Scarbro ou de Brooklyn; et leurs railways flanquent,
creusent, surplombent les dispositions de cet Hôtel,
choisies dans l'histoire des plus élégantes et des plus
colossales constructions de l'Italie, de l'Amérique et de
l'Asie, dont les fenêtres et les terrasses à présent pleines
d'éclairages, de boissons et de brises riches, sont ouvertes
à l'esprit des voyageurs et des nobles — qui permettent,
aux heures du jour, à toutes les tarentelles des côtes, —
et même aux ritournelles des vallées illustres de l'art, de
décorer merveilleusement les façades du Palais-Promon-
toire.

HEADLAND

Golden dawn and shimmering evening find our brig at sea opposite this villa and its dependencies which form a headland as extensive as Epirus and the Peloponnesos, or as the large island of Japan, or as Arabia! Temples lighted up by the return of Greek boats; tremendous views of modern coastal defenses; dunes illuminated by hot flowers and bacchanales; grand canals of Carthage and Embankments of a doubtful Venice; lazy eruptions of Etnas and gullies full of flowers and glacier waters; laundries surrounded by German poplars; strange hilly parks leaning out of the tops of Japanese trees; and circular facades of the "Grands" and the "Royals" of Scarborough and of Brooklyn; and their railways flank, hollow out, and dominate this hotel chosen from among the most elegant and the most colossal buildings of Italy, America, and Asia and whose windows and balconies, now full of illuminations and drinks and heavy breezes, invite the comments of travelers and aristocrats — who permit, by daylight, all the tarantellas of the coast — and even the ritournellas of the illustrious valleys of Art — to decorate the facades of Headland Palace, *marvelously.*

V
VISIONARY LIFE

"The Poet makes himself a SEER by a long,
immense, and reasoned DERANGEMENT
OF ALL THE SENSES. All forms of love,
suffering, and madness; he explores himself,
he tries out all the poisons on himself and
keeps only their quintessences. Unspeakable
torture where he really needs faith, all the
superhuman strength there is, where he
becomes in the midst of everyone else the
great sick man, the great criminal, the
great condemned — and the supreme
Knower! — since he has reached the UN-
KNOWN!"

Letter to Paul Demeny
(Charleville, May 1871).

DÉPART

Assez vu. La vision s'est rencontrée à tous les airs.

Assez eu. Rumeurs des villes, le soir, et au soleil, et toujours.

Assez connu. Les arrêts de la vie. — O Rumeurs et Visions!

Départ dans l'affection et le bruit neufs.

CUTTING OUT

Seen enough. The vision bumped into in season and out.

Had enough. Racket of cities, at evening. and in sunlight, and always.

Known enough. The let-downs of life. — O Rumblings and Visions!

Cutting out to New Feelings, New Sounds!

ROYAUTÉ

Un beau matin, chez un peuple fort doux, un homme et
une femme superbes criaient sur la place publique :
« Mes amis, je veux qu'elle soit reine! » « Je veux
être reine! » Elle riait et tremblait. Il parlait aux amis
de révélation, d'épreuve terminée. Ils se pâmaient l'un
contre l'autre.

En effet, ils furent rois toute une matinée, où les
tentures carminées se relevèrent sur les maisons, et toute
l'aprés-midi, où ils s'avancèrent du côté des jardins de
palmes.

ROYALTY

One fine morning, in a land of extremely gentle people,
a very beautiful man and woman called out, quite loud,
in a public place: "Dear friends, I want her to be queen!"
"And I want to *be* queen!" She was laughing, trembling.
He was telling friends about a revelation, about an *ordeal*
they'd come through. They were weak with happiness.

As a matter of fact, they *were* royalty for a whole
morning, while the houses were covered with bright-red
bunting, and for a whole afternoon, while they walked
in the direction of the palm gardens.

A UNE RAISON

Un coup de ton doigt sur le tambour décharge tous les sons et commence la nouvelle harmonie.

Un pas de toi c'est la levée des nouveaux hommes et leur en marche.

Ta tête se détourne : le nouvel amour! Ta tête se retourne : — le nouvel amour!

« Change nos lots, crible les fléaux, à commencer par le temps », te chantent ces enfants.
« Élève n'importe où la substance de nos fortunes et de nos voeux », on t'en prie.

Arrivée de toujours, qui t'en iras partout.

TO SOME GOD

One tap of your little finger on the drum lets out the New Sound and the New Harmony's here!

One step by you and the new men are standing tall and ready to go.

Your head turns one way: a new kind of love! Your head turns another way: a new kind of love!

"Change our life, rid us of the plague, start with Time," these children cry out to you. "Bring about ANYWHERE AT ALL the reality of good times and wishes come true," they beg you.

Arrived from *all the time,* aboard for *all there is!*

MYSTIQUE

Sur la pente du talus, les anges tournent leurs robes de laine, dans les herbages d'acier et d'émeraude.

Des prés de flammes bondissent jusqu'au sommet du mamelon. A gauche, le terreau de l'arête est piétiné par tous les homicides et toutes les batailles, et tous les bruits désastreux filent leur courbe. Derrière l'arête de droite, la ligne des orients, des progrès.

Et, tandis que la bande, en haut du tableau, est formée de la rumeur tournante et bondissante des conques des mers et des nuits humaines,

La douceur fleurie des étoiles et du ciel et du reste descend en face du talus, comme un panier, contre notre face, et fait l'abîme fleurant et bleu là-dessous.

MYSTIC

On the slope of the hill the angels whirl their woolen robes in grasses of steel and emerald.

Meadows of flame leap up to the top of the little hill. On the left, the earth of the ridge has been trampled on by all the murderers and all the battles, and all the sounds of disaster flare up in their orbit. Behind the ridge on the right, the line of the Orient, of movements.

And whereas the band at the top of the picture is made up of whirling and leaping uproars of seashells and mortal nights.

The flowering sweetness of stars and sky and the rest falls across the slope, like a basket, before our faces, and makes the abyss all flowers and blue beneath.

VEILLÉES

I

C'est le repos éclairé, ni fièvre ni langueur, sur le lit ou sur le pré.

C'est l'ami ni ardent ni faible. L'ami.

C'est l'aimée ni tourmentante ni tourmentée. L'aimée.

L'air et le monde point cherchés. La vie.

— Etait-ce donc ceci?

— Et le rêve fraîchit.

II

L'éclairage revient à l'arbre de bâtisse. Des deux extrémités de la salle, décors quelconques, des élévations harmoniques se joignent. La muraille en face du veilleur est une succession psychologique de coupes de frises, de bandes atmosphériques et d'accidences géologiques. — Rêve intense et rapide de groupes sentimentaux avec des êtres de tous les caractères parmi toutes les apparences.

NIGHT-WATCHES

I

It's time out in the light, with no fever and no faintness, on a bed or in a field.

It's the buddy with no violence and no weakness. The buddy.

It's the girl friend with no sadistic cravings and no bad memories. The girl friend.

Air and a world not striven for. The life.

— Was this really IT?

— And the dream cooled off.

II

The lighting comes back to the high beam. From the two opposite ends of the room, decorations — nothing special, harmonic highs *combining.* The wall opposite the onlooker is a psychological sequence of breaks, friezes, atmospheric bands, and geological accidents — Intense, fast-moving dream of emotional groupings with people of all conceivable kinds in the thick of appearances.

III

Les lampes et les tapis de la veillée font le bruit des vagues, la nuit, le long de la coque et autour du steerage.

La mer de la veillée, telle que les seins d'Amélie.

Les tapisseries, jusqu'à mi-hauteur, des taillis de dentelle, teinte d'émeraude, où se jettent les tourterelles de la veillée.

*

La plaque du foyer noir, de réels soleils des grèves : ah! puits des magies; seule vue d'aurore, cette fois.

III

The lamps and rugs of this watch make the sounds of waves, in the night, along the keel and around the steerage deck.

The sea of the night-watch, like the titties of Emily.

The tapestries, halfway up, undergrowths of emerald-tainted lace, where the doves of the night-watch fling themselves.

*

Smutchy back-wall of the fireplace, real suns on real seashores! Ah! wells of magic. Mere glimpse of dawn, that time.

SOIR HISTORIQUE

En quelque soir, par exemple, que se trouve le touriste naïf, retiré de nos horreurs économiques, la main d'un maître anime le clavecin des prés; on joue aux cartes au fond de l'étang, miroir évocateur des reines et des mignonnes; on a les saintes, les voiles, et les fils d'harmonie, et les chromatismes légendaires, sur le couchant.

Il frissonne au passage des chasses et des hordes. La comédie goutte sur les tréteaux de gazon. Et l'embarras des pauvres et des faibles sur ces plans stupides!

A sa vision esclave, l'Allemagne s'échafaude vers des lunes; les déserts tartares s'éclairent; les révoltes anciennes grouillent dans le centre du Céleste Empire; par les escaliers et les fauteuils de rocs, un petit monde blême et plat, Afrique et Occidents, va s'édifier. Puis un ballet de mers et de nuits connues, une chimie sans valeur, et des mélodies impossibles.

La même magie bourgeoise à tous les points où la malle nous déposera! Le plus élémentaire physicien sent qu'il n'est plus possible de se soumettre à cette atmosphère personnelle, brume de remords physiques, dont la constatation est déjà une affliction.

Non! Le moment de l'étuve, des mers enlevées, des embrasements souterrains, de la planète emportée, et des exterminations conséquentes, certitudes si peu malignement indiquées dans la Bible et par les Nornes et qu'il sera donné à l'être sérieux de surveiller. — Cependant ce ne sera point un effet de légende!

HISTORIC EVENING

On some evening. for instance, when the unsophisti-
cated tourist has retired from our economic nightmares,
a master's hand makes the harpsichord of the fields come
alive; they're playing cards at the bottom of the pool, a
mirror which brings to mind a few queens and call-girls;
they've got saints, veils, threads of harmony, and many-
colored legends out there in the sunset.

He shivers at the passing of hunts and hordes. Comedy
drips onto the stages of grass. And the shyness of the
weak and the poor in these stupid arrangements!

Before his slaves's vision, Germany is scaffolding itself
toward some moons; Tartar deserts are lighting up;
ancient revolts are rumbling in the center of the Celestial
Empire; over stairways and armchairs of rock, a weak and
flat little world, Africa and Occidents, will be built up.
Then a ballet of well-known seas and nights, a worthless
chemistry, and impossible melodies.

The same middle-class magic wherever the mail train
drops you off! The most elementary physicist feels it's no
longer possible to put up with this *personalized* atmos-
phere, this thickness of physical remorse, which is a
headache to even think about.

No! the time of the cauldron, of seas swept aside, of
underground fire-storms, of the planet blown away and
the resulting exterminations, certainties indicated with
so little malice by the Bible and the Nornes and which
serious persons would do well to prepare for. — Yet it'll
be nothing to make legends of!

MOUVEMENT

Le mouvement de lacet sur la berge des chutes du
    fleuve,
Le gouffre à l'étambot,
La célérite de la rampe,
L'énorme passade du courant
Mènent par les lumières inouïes
Et la nouveauté chimique
Les voyageurs entourés des trompes du val
Et du strom.

Ce sont les conquérants du monde
Cherchant la fortune chimique personnelle;
Le sport et le comfort voyagent avec eux;
Ils emmènent l'éducation
Des races, des classes et des bêtes, sur ce vaisseau
Repos et vertige
A la lumière diluvienne,
Aux terribles soirs d'étude.

Car de la causerie parmi les appareils, le sang, les
    fleurs, le feu, les bijoux,
Des comptes agités à ce bord fuyard,
— On voit, roulant comme une digue au delà de la
    route hydraulique motrice,

Monstrueux, s'éclairant sans fin, — leur stock d'études;
Eux chassés dans l'extase harmonique,
Et l'héroïsme de la découverte.
Aux accidents atmosphériques les plus surprenants,
Un couple de jeunesse s'isole sur l'arche
— Est-ce ancienne sauvagerie qu'on pardonne? —
Et chante et se poste.

MOVEMENT

The rhythmic movement on the river falls' bank,
The whirlpool at the sternpost,
The swiftness of the hand-rail,
And the huge passing of the current
Conduct through unheard-of lights
And a chemical newness
The voyagers surrounded by the waterspouts of the
    valley
And the strøm.

These are the conquerors of the world
Seeking a personal chemical fortune;
Sports and comforts travel along with them;
They bring the eduction
Of races, classes, and animals, on this boat,
Repose and vertigo
To this diluvian light,
To terrible nights of study.

Since from the talk among the apparatus, the blood, the
    flowers, the fire, the jewels,
From the agitated counting aboard this fugitive ship,
 — You can see, rolling like a dyke beyond the hydrau-
lic power road,
Monstrous, endlessly illuminated — their stock of
    studies;
Themselves hunted into harmonic ecstasy,
And the heroism of discovery.
During the most unbelievable incidental transactions,
A young couple moves apart at a bridge
 — Is it an ancient savagery that has to be forgiven? —
And sings and *stands pat.*

GÉNIE

Il est l'affection et le présent puisqu'il a fait la maison ouverte à l'hiver écumeux et à la rumeur de l'été, lui qui a purifié les boissons et les aliments, lui qui est le charme des lieux fuyants et le délice surhumain des stations. Il est l'affection et l'avenir, la force et l'amour que nous, debout dans les rages et les ennuis, nous voyons passer dans le ciel de tempête et les drapeaux d'extase.

Il est l'amour, mesure parfaite et réinventée, raison merveilleuse et imprévue, et l'éternité : machine aimée des qualités fatales. Nous avons tous eu l'épouvante de sa concession et de la nôtre : ô jouissance de notre santé, élan de nos facultés, affection égoïste et passion pour lui, lui qui nous aime pour sa vie infinie . . .

Et nous nous le rappelons et il voyage . . . Et si l'Adoration s'en va, sonne, sa promesse sonne : « Arrière ces superstitions, ces anciens corps, ces ménages et ces âges. C'est cette époque-ci qui a sombré! »

Il ne s'en ira pas, il ne redescendra pas d'un ciel, il n'accomplira pas la rédemption des colères de femmes et des gaietés des hommes et de tout ce Péché : car c'est fait, lui étant, et étant aimé.

O ses souffles, ses têtes, ses courses; la terrible célérité de la perfection des formes et de l'action!

O fécondité de l'esprit et immensité de l'univers!

Son corps! Le dégagement rêvé, le brisement de la grâce croisée de violence nouvelle!

Sa vue, sa vue! tous les agenouillages anciens et les peines *relevées* à sa suite.

Son jour! l'abolition de toutes souffrances sonores et mouvantes dans la musique plus intense.

Son pas! les migrations plus énormes que les anciennes invasions.

O lui et nous! l'orgueil plus bienveillant que les charités perdues.

GENIUS

He's FEELINGS and he's NOW because he's held open house for the heady blizzards of winter as well as summertime's easy rap-sessions — he's unpolluted our food and drink — he's the magus of running away and the not-quite-human bliss of standing still. He's feelings and the FUTURE, the heart and energy we see passing overhead between the storms and the streamers of ecstasy, as we stand pat in our boredoms and rages.

He's love, the perfect measure invented from scratch, the marvelous and unthinkable logic, and eternity: the instrument loved strictly for its fatality. We've all known terror of his allowance and our own: the thrill of good health, the pleasuring of the senses, the ego-centered lust and the wild craving for him — who loves us as long as his life, without end.

And we call him to mind and he's traveling . . . And if Adoration goes, rings, his *promise* rings: "Down with these superstitions, these wrinkled bodies, these couples and old ages. THIS is the age that's *failed!*"

O his breaths, his heads, his races: the tremendous quickness of flawless forms and flawless action!

O inventiveness of the mind and fullness of the universe!

His body! the dreamed-of liberation, the thrashing of loveliness matched with new violence! the sight of him, the *sight!* all the old boot-licking and the penalties NULL AND VOID when he comes.

His day! the abolition of all blatant and restless sufferings in music more intense.

His step! migrations more far-ranging than the invasions of early times.

O he and us! pride more largehearted than the lost charities.

O monde! et le chant clair des malheurs nouveaux!

Il nous a connus tous et nous a tous aimés. Sachons, cette nuit d'hiver, de cap en cap, du pôle tumultueux au château, de la foule à la plage, de regards en regards, forces et sentiments las, le héler et le voir et, le renvoyer et, sous les marées et au haut des déserts de neige, suivre ses vues, ses souffles, son corps, son jour.

O world! and the clear sounds of up-to-date miseries.
He's known all of us and has loved us all: let's, this
winter night, from Cape to Cape, from the uproarious
pole to the castle, from the crowd to the beach, from look
to look, our energies at low ebb, ANNOUNCE him and
SEE him, and send him on his way, and down under
tides and high in deserts of snow, go after his sight —
his breath — his body — his day —

DÉVOTIONS

A ma soeur Louise Vanaen de Voringhem : — Sa cornette bleue tournée à la mer du Nord. — Pour les naufragés.

A ma soeur Léonie Aubois d'Ashby. Baou! — l'herbe d'été bourdonnante et puante. — Pour la fièvre des mères et des enfants.

A Lulu, — démon — qui a conservé un goût pour les oratoires du temps des Amies et de son éducation incomplète. — Pour les hommes. A madame ***

A l'adolescent que je fus. A ce saint vieillard, ermitage ou mission.

A l'esprit des pauvres. Et à un très haut clergé.

Aussi bien à tout culte en telle place de culte mémoriale et parmi tels événements qu'il faille se rendre, suivant les aspirations du moment ou bien notre propre vice sérieux.
Ce soir, à Circeto des hautes glaces, grasse comme le poisson, et enluminée comme les dix mois de la nuit rouge — (son coeur ambre et spunk), — pour ma seule prière muette comme ces régions de nuit et précédant des bravoures plus violentes que ce chaos polaire.

A tout prix et avec tous les airs, même dans des voyages métaphysiques. — Mais plus *alors*.

DEVOTIONS

To Sister Louise Vanaen de Voringhem: — Her blue coif turned toward the North Sea. — Pray for the shipwrecked.

To Sister Léonie Aubois d'Ashby, woof! — the buzzing, stinking summer grass. — Pray for the fever of mothers and children.

To Lulu — devil — who has retained a taste for oratories of the time of the Friends and her unfinished education. — Pray for men. To Madame***

To the adolescent I once was. To that holy old man, hermitage or mission.

To the smartness of the poor. And to an extremely high clergy.

As well as to all cults in every place of traditional worship and to whatever events one must take part in according to the aspirations of the moment or else to one's own special vice.

This evening to Cicerto of the lofty ices, fat as fish, and illuminated like the ten months of the scarlet night — (her heart amber and spunky) — for my only prayer silent like these regions of night, and coming before bravuras more violent than this polar chaos.

At all costs, in season and out, even in metaphysical journeys. — But no more THEN.

SOLDE

A vendre ce que les Juifs n'ont pas vendu, ce que noblesse ni crime n'ont goûté, ce qu'ignore l'amour maudit et la probité infernale des masses; ce que le temps ni la science n'ont pas à reconnaître :

Les Voix reconstituées; l'éveil fraternel de toutes les énergies chorales et orchestrales et leurs applications instantanées; l'occasion, unique, de dégager nos sens!

A vendre les Corps sans prix, hors de toute race, de tout monde, de tout sexe, de toute descendance! Les richesses jaillissant à chaque démarche! Solde de diamants sans contrôle!

A vendre l'anarchie pour les masses; la satisfaction irrépressible pour les amateurs supérieurs; la mort atroce pour les fidèles et les amants!

A vendre les habitations et les migrations, sports, féeries et conforts parfaits, et le bruit, le mouvement et l'avenir qu'ils font!

A vendre les applications de calcul et les sauts d'harmonie inouïs. Les trouvailles et les termes non soupçonnés, possession immédiate.

Élan insensé et infini aux splendeurs invisibles, aux délices insensibles, — et ses secrets affolants pour chaque vice — et sa gaîté effrayante pour la foule.

A vendre les corps, les voix, l'immense opulence inquestionable, ce qu'on ne vendra jamais. Les vendeurs ne sont pas à bout de solde! Les voyageurs n'ont pas à rendre leur commission de si tôt!

CLEARANCE SALE

For sale what the Jews weren't able to sell, what even the upper crust and the gangsters have never been treated to, what's not known in the most repulsive of sexual practices or in the most damnable uprightness of the masses, what neither Time nor Science need give their seal of approval to —:

Re-serviced Voices: the human re-conditioning of all choral and instrumental energies and their immediate putting to use — a once-in-a-lifetime opportunity to free our senses!

For sale priceless Bodies, without regard to race, world, breed, or sex! Bargains galore in all departments! Unrestricted sale of diamonds!

For sale Anarchy for the masses: satisfaction *guaranteed* to those who know the score. Unbeatable deaths for the steady customers and the lovers.

For sale fine old homes and migrations, sports, fairy-lands, and perfect comfort, with all the noise, the movement, and the future that go with them!

For sale shipments of calculations and truly remarkable harmonic progressions. Discoveries and terminologies like you've never *dared dream of.* Immediate delivery.

Wild, round-the-clock in-rushes to invisible splendors, to intangible delights — with their delirious secrets for every perversion — and their terrifying gaiety for the in-rushing crowds.

For sale the Bodies, the beautiful Voices, the immense and unquestionable Affluence, what can never be sold out. The salesmen have barely begun to touch the stock! No need for travelers to turn in their orders *so soon!*

Bertrand Mathieu was born in Lewiston, Maine — just up the road a piece from Lisbon, Maine, where the Editor/ Publisher of BOA Editions was born. He has lived and traveled widely in Germany, Italy, Yugoslavia, Greece, Turkey, Mexico, and the American Southwest, where he earned a Ph.D. in English at the University of Arizona (Tucson) in 1975.

Mathieu spent most of the summer of 1978 tramping through Brittany, Provence, Normandy, and the Ardennes, especially in Charleville, the hometown of Arthur Rimbaud, where he did research for his forthcoming translations of Rimbaud's boyhood poems.

In addition to a new American translation of Rimbaud's *A Season in Hell* (Pomegranate, 1977, with a preface by Anaïs Nin and etchings by Jim Dine), Mathieu also has published a volume of poems, *Landscape with Voices* (Delta, 1965), and a critical study entitled *Orpheus in Brooklyn: Orphism, Rimbaud, and Henry Miller* (Mouton, 1976). He is presently completing a critical study of the work of Anaïs Nin entitled *Freeing Eurydice: Rimbaud, Anaïs Nin and the Gnostic Outlook,* with a preface by Lawrence Durrell.

Bertrand Mathieu's poems, translations, reviews, and critical essays have appeared in *American Poetry Review, City Lights Anthology, Essays in Arts and Sciences, Chicago Review, Concerning Poetry, Partisan Review, Poetry,* and *The Village Voice.* A former Woodrow Wilson Fellow and the recipient of grants from the National Endowment for the Humanities and the Lilly Foundation at Yale University, Mathieu is Professor of English at the University of New Haven. He lives in New Haven with his son, Russell, a student at the University of Connecticut, and his daughter, Rachel, a student at Richard C. Lee High School.

Illuminations has been issued in a first edition of twelve hundred copies. Seven hundred and fifty copies are in paper and four hundred copies are in cloth. Fifty additional copies have been specially bound by Gene Eckert in quarter cloth and French papers over boards; ten copies are numbered I-X signed by Bertrand Mathieu and Henry Miller and include an original pen-and-ink drawing by Henry Miller; twenty-six copies are lettered A-Z and are signed by Bertrand Mathieu and Henry Miller; fourteen copies, numbered i-xiv, signed by Bertrand Mathieu and Henry Miller have been retained for presentation purposes.